ISIS' Propaganda Machine

This book examines ISIS' media propaganda machine.

The book focuses on case studies that have been largely understudied in relation to ISIS' media production. Empirically, it offers new insights into how ISIS uses its media production to disseminate its extremist ideology by focusing on video games, educational apps, Dark Web sites, and offline billboards. The book argues that despite all the discussion about how ISIS has disappeared or even died, the terrorist group's daily activities on the Dark Web show that they are still thriving and disseminating their propaganda in more than 20 different languages, and effectively functioning as an international news organization. Using a mixed-method research approach, the book offers a multilayered understanding of media content and fills a major gap in the literature, especially in relation to the use of educational apps and the Dark Web.

This book will be of much interest to students of media and communication studies, terrorism and counterterrorism, Middle Eastern politics, and international relations.

Ahmed Al-Rawi is Associate Professor of News, Social Media, and Public Communication at the School of Communication at Simon Fraser University, Canada, and author of eight books, including, most recently, *Cyberwars in the Middle East* (2021).

ISIS' Propaganda Machine

Global Mediated Terrorism

Ahmed Al-Rawi

LONDON AND NEW YORK

First published 2024
by Routledge
4 Park Square, Milton Park, Abingdon, Oxon OX14 4RN

and by Routledge
605 Third Avenue, New York, NY 10158

Routledge is an imprint of the Taylor & Francis Group, an informa business

British Library Cataloguing-in-Publication Data
A catalogue record for this book is available from the British Library

ISBN: 978-1-032-61586-8 (hbk)
ISBN: 978-1-032-61587-5 (pbk)
ISBN: 978-1-032-61588-2 (ebk)

DOI: 10.4324/9781032615882

Typeset in Galliard
by Newgen Publishing UK

Contents

Introduction

This book focuses on case studies that have been largely understudied in relation to the Islamic State in Iraq and Syria's (ISIS') propaganda. Empirically, it offers new insights into how ISIS uses its media production to disseminate its extremist ideology by focusing on video games, Twitter (now 'X'), educational apps, Dark Web, and street billboards. Despite all the discussion on how ISIS has disappeared or even died, the Dark Website analysis shows that the terrorist group is still thriving and disseminating its propaganda in more than 20 different languages, functioning as an international news organization.

This book is divided into five core chapters, an introduction, and a conclusion. Each chapter deals with one form of ISIS' media propaganda, and I have arranged them to show the evolution of the medium and the message. Chapter 1, for example, explores the issue of offline communication applied in ISIS' previously controlled territories, in which I focus on the systematic analysis of street billboards and how promotional leaflets were used. Using thematic analysis, I categorize these billboards into nine themes, and the prevalent ones include promoting ISIS' sharia law, calls for jihad, stressing women's garment and behavior, and discussing ISIS as a functional state. I argue that these offline propaganda publications assisted the terrorist group in promoting its nation-state building goals.

Chapter 2 revolves around the use of social media by ISIS members and their sympathizers. Unlike the first chapter, which stresses the importance of centralized media productions, we see noncentralized control and operations on social media due to the

DOI: 10.4324/9781032615882-1

nature of social networks that allow everyone to participate. As a result, there is more noise on social media, but important insight can still be gleaned. Using a mixed-method approach, I employed big data analysis to extract relevant small amount of content after which a qualitative study was conducted. I mostly explored the way some Arabic-language users directed their attacks against Al-Qaeda terrorist group and especially its leader, Ayman Al-Zawahri.

The Chapter 3 deals with the use of video games in the promotion of terrorism, especially that which targets younger people. Here, we witness a linear development, which I term 'Jihad 3.0', whose main aims are related to gaining more publicity and attention. Similar to social media, the video game 'Salil al-Sawarem' ('The Clanging of the Swords'), can be considered another non-centralized media production that is developed by some of ISIS' sympathizers. To better understand the game, I focus on its audience reception on YouTube by systemically analyzing the comments on the videos discussing it. Though there were not many supporters of the game, the pro-ISIS users formed a strong online community that used trolling and flaming techniques to silence critics.

Chapter 4 delves into another development in ISIS' media strategy which is connected to its educational mobile apps. Using the Walkthrough method, I investigate four apps targeting children, and I argue that the terrorist group developed these tools to enhance its nation-state building activities, influence children's understanding of Islam, and promote its terrorist ideology, especially the focus on militarized violence. Similar to the billboards that are discussed in Chapter 1, these apps are centralized media productions.

Finally, Chapter 5 offers new insight about the latest development in the terrorist group's propaganda, which is the use of the Dark Web. After identifying four Dark Web sites, I used a mixed-method approach to offer a multilayered understanding of ISIS' multimodal messages, including the analysis of its news images. Though not all the websites are directly run by ISIS' media apparatus, at least one of them, i3lam, is a centralized media site on which daily updates are offered, especially regarding terrorist activities in Western Africa. Because ISIS is largely blocked on the surface web, I argue that the Dark Web and to a lesser extent

Telegram offer a lifeline to the terrorist group, allowing it to get funding and connect with its members and sympathizers.

Theoretically, all the chapters of this book are situated within the concept of propaganda, and three other chapters, including those on billboards, the Dark Web, and apps, are also discussed within the conceptual framework of state-nation building efforts and Anderson's 'imagined communities' due to their standardized and centralized media productions. I argue in this work that in its utopian objective in creating a nation-state, ISIS attempted to establish an imagined nation-state, especially that one of its goals was to demolish the Sykes-Picot Agreement in 1916 and any available secular laws in the Middle East and North Africa (MENA) region. This introduction offers the readers a theoretical framework about propaganda and the concept of nation-state building, while the conclusion sums up the major findings of the study and provides suggestions for future research.

In general, ISIS is known to be more militant and dangerous than Al-Qaeda as it has evolved to be a hybrid group that mixes between strict and deviant versions of Wahhabism and Salafism. Shortly after its spread, ISIS declared itself a so-called 'state', especially after controlling large areas in Syria and Iraq. Other remote militant groups in other regions like in Libya and Nigeria pledged allegiance to Abu Bakr Al-Baghdadi, making ISIS extend its geographical outreach. Indeed, this self-proclaimed jihadist nation-state, in itself, became an appealing feature that can draw recruits to join and become part of this alleged utopian notion.

According to a senior leading figure in this terrorist group, the ideological foundation of ISIS was established in Camp Bucca, which was the largest US detention facility in Iraq. Due to the time prisoners spent at the Camp and the fact that many other insurgent members were detained there, it became a fertile ground for extremism wherein Islamists managed to hold numerous meetings and make detailed agreements for future plans (Chulov, 2014). When ISIS advanced in the Sunni provinces, it looted banks and became the richest terrorist group in the world (Tait, 2014). It also committed war crimes as hundreds of captured Iraqi soldiers, especially Shiites, were executed, while the Yezihdi and Christian minorities suffered a great deal as many were forced to flee to Iraqi Kurdistan (CBS, 2014; Spencer, 2014).

In this respect, ISIS was successful in recruitment, since one of its most important appeals being employed was its professed link to a conservative version of Islam (Salaf, or pious predecessors). This claim was used as a marketing tool by ISIS as its members insist on utilizing the black banner which was originally used by Muslims when Islam first emerged. Further, the group's name itself is meant to sound Islamic (ISIS), or later abbreviated as the Islamic State (Tandheem Al-Dawlah Al-Islamiah). Third, there was an ongoing flow of information from cities controlled by ISIS, showing that the group intended to rule in a utopian way, allegedly reminiscent of early Islam, especially in relation to highlighting religious duties and obligations. The above claims were all meant to brand ISIS as a purely Islamic group, so any attack against its members is regarded as an attack against Islam itself. For example, ISIS' *Dabiq* magazine refers to anyone that fights the group as an enemy of Islam, infidel, or apostate. In an article on Abu Sinan al-Najdi, who was killed in his attack on the Al Salul Emergency Task Force in Saudi Arabia, the writer pledges revenge against Saudi security forces:

> By Allah! You will not enjoy safety and security, and you will not have a comfortable life as long as you wage war against Islam and the Muslims and remain as tails of the West, which plays around with you as it pleases. Your coalition with the Majus [pejorative for Shiites] and the Crusaders against Ahlus-Sunnah [Sunnis] in Iraq and Shām is the biggest witness against you.
>
> (Dabiq, 2015, p. 35)

Further, ISIS repeatedly portrays itself as an alleged protector of Sunni Islam while the theme of victimhood in the sense that Muslims, especially Sunnis, are victims of world powers is prominent in ISIS' promotional materials, as explained in some chapters of this book. Indeed, equating the group with Islam and the Sunni faith was one of the appeals that drives some devout Muslims to join this criminal and terrorist organization.

This study builds upon earlier work that examined propaganda audiovisual productions and social media use of ISIS (Stern & Berger, 2015). The terrorist group used to run a sophisticated and centralized media apparatus with its own news agency called Amaq (depths), *Dabiq* magazine in Arabic and English, as well as the Al-Bayan radio station in Mosul that also featured a mobile app (Callimachi, 2016). In its self-identified jihad, previous work has shown that ISIS views media as an important tool to brand itself and promote the group's extremist ideology. It is important to note here that the shocking beheading and killing images and videos disseminated by ISIS were meant to create awareness about the group and its activities similar to the shock advertising techniques used by some commercial corporations; this aspect of advertising impact is well documented in previous scientific research (Dahl, Frankenberger, & Manchanda, 2003; Chan et al., 2007; Dens, De Pelsmacker, & Janssens, 2008; Jones, Cunningham, & Gallagher, 2010; Nelson-Field, Riebe, & Newstead, 2013). These shocking images were used as another persuasive strategy as ISIS attempts to brand itself as a savage group that is allegedly defending Islam against the infidels, represented by anyone that fights them. In this regard, social networking sites are mostly used to attract attention and entice possible victims, after which other communication technologies are used, especially mobile services like Viber, Surespot, WhatsApp, FaceTime, Kik, Skype, and Telegram (Siemaszko, 2014; James, 2015; Jaffer, 2015; Callimachi, 2015). In brief, the different platforms used and media strategies followed by ISIS, which seem to complement each other, indicate that the group was waging a new jihad that went beyond what Web 2.0 offered, making it far more effective than traditional terrorist organizations like Al-Qaeda.

In the following section, a theoretical discussion is provided on the concept of propaganda in the contemporary online ecosystem with a focus on ISIS' vision of media and e-jihad.

Jihad and Propaganda

Before discussing ISIS and its online media strategies, a review on the connection between terrorism and propaganda is provided. Jowett and O'Donnell define propaganda as the 'deliberate, systematic attempt to shape perceptions, manipulate cognitions, and divert behavior to achieve a response that furthers the desired intent of the propagandist' (2012, p. 7). Indeed, media can be used as a tool by terrorists to spread fear 'and an uncertain future' (Altheide, 2007, p. 287). Weimann mentions that terrorism and propaganda are closely connected, for:

> terrorists see the media as a powerful tool in their psychological warfare… They can use terrorist attacks to promote their cause on the media agenda and thus on the public agenda, they can turn to their own people seeking legitimacy, support, and funding and even recruit new members.
>
> (2005, p. 383)

Many scholars argue that there is a symbiotic relationship between media and terrorism due to their mutual dependence on each other as terrorists 'thrive on the oxygen of publicity' (Wilkinson, 1997). In other words, without media coverage and propaganda, the impact of the terrorists' action and their imagined and real influence cannot be noticed by the public. Schmid and de Graaf state that 'an act of terrorism is in reality an act of communication' (1982, p. 14). Similarly, Freedman and Thussu believe that media outlets are at the core of terrorism because they are 'increasingly seen as active agents in the actual conceptualization of terrorist events' (2012, p. 10). As will be discussed throughout the chapters of this book, ISIS fully exploits various media platforms in order to disseminate fearful propaganda messages and create an effective impact on their receivers.

Hence, many scholars have argued that terrorism is 'propaganda of the deed' (Bueno de Mesquita & Dickson, 2007) whose original concept was developed by three Italian anarchists (Errico Malatesta, Carlo Cafiero, and Emilio Covelli) in the late 19th century. In fact, terrorism is often defined as

> an act of propaganda. The terrorist act, in and of itself, communicates that change can occur and the violence of the act commands the attention of the society. The propaganda effect is in the act of securing the attention of the populous and then providing the message through the violence.
>
> (Garrison, 2004, p. 265)

For the terrorist group, violent acts are symbolic as they are meant to send different messages beyond the creation of fear, hence the term 'terrorism of the spectacle' (Baudrillard & Valentin, 2002, p. 15). Walter Laqueur observes that the 'success of a terrorist operation depends almost entirely on the amount of publicity it receives' (as cited in Schmid, 2005, p. 141) which explains why terrorists groups find it imperative to actively spread information about their ideology and various activities along many media outlets, especially social media. The ultimate main objectives of using propaganda are to create fear, mobilize people to support the terrorist's cause, and disrupt their opponents' efforts (Wilkinson, 1997). Since the modern media era, propaganda has been utilized as a mobilization tool by a wide range of organizations (Wright, 1991; Paletz & Schmid, 1992; Nacos, 1994), and ISIS has invested heavily in the use of propaganda. From its early emergence, ISIS has become well known for using various propaganda methods and approaches to brand itself to the world in different languages (Farwell, 2014; Neer & O'Toole, 2014). As such, ISIS cultivated an online media strategy that has been labeled Jihad 3.0 (Al-Rawi, 2016) due to its highly sophisticated media campaign that involves the use of multilayered propaganda such as high-tech filming and editing equipment. There is also evidence that suggests that a number of ISIS' operations in some countries have been funded by Bitcoin transactions done on the Dark Web (McCoy, 2017), and Chapter 5 offers an in-depth analysis on this online site.

To understand ISIS' media strategy, it is vital to provide some historical insights into some Islamic terrorist groups such as Al-Qaeda terrorist group; some of the documents retrieved from Bin Laden's compound in Abbottabad demonstrate his emphasis on the role of online media, stating 'media occupies the greater portion of the battle today'. Further, in a letter he sent in 2002 to the Taliban leader, Mullah Omar, Bin Laden said, 'It is obvious that the media war in this century is one of the strongest methods; in fact, its ratio may reach 90 percent of the total preparation for the battles' (as cited in Klausen, 2015). Similarly, al-Zawahiri, mentioned once that 'We are in a battle, and more than half of this battle is taking place in the battlefield of the media', while the American jihadist Omar Hammami, who was one of the leaders of al-Shabab terrorist group, declared that 'The war of narratives has become even more important than the war of navies, napalm, and knives' (Cottee, 2015).

To achieve the jihadist goals, one of the main platforms used to influence people is social media. In fact, some scholars believe that social media could become instrumental in sometimes radicalizing some members of the public in relation to broader political and social issues (Dahlberg, 2007). Al-Qaeda, for example, has been active on many online forums for several years waging an e-jihad to recruit sympathizers and spread its ideology (Conway & McInerney, 2008; Ali Musawi, 2010). It also created a 'jihadist cloud' which allowed it to maintain 'its virtual spaces and niches on the Internet' (Prucha, 2011). These (offline) extremist groups use modern technology and the Internet as the main means to influence others. 'For the terrorists themselves, new media are, collectively, a transformative tool that offers endless possibilities for communication and expansion' (Seib & Janbek, 2011, p. ix). In this regard, there are different psychological motivations that lead some individuals to join extremist groups that can be categorized as 'revenge seekers [who] need an outlet for their frustration, status seekers [who] need recognition, identity seekers [who] need a group to join, and thrill seekers [who] need adventure' (Venhaus, 2010).

One of the earliest works that assisted in founding the ideological foundations of ISIS was Abu Bakr Naji's 'The Administration of Savagery' which was posted online around 2004 (Wright, 2006; Naji, 2006). In this work, Abu Bakr Naji defines the jihadist struggles as 'media battles' (2006, p. 73) and repeatedly mentions the term 'deceptive media halo' that is undertaken by ISIS' opponents in order to 'falsely' persuade the masses that jihad is a wrong practice. Naji is deeply critical of Al-Qaeda for stressing the need to address the elites and ignoring the masses (al-awam) who should have been given more emphasis. He stresses the need to establish a media division 'whose purpose is to communicate what we want to say to the masses and focus their attention on it, even if this requires exposing the group to danger that is comparable to the danger of a military operation' (pp. 95–96).

Here, Naji affirms that members of the general public have to be persuaded first, stressing that the 'role of media politics is to gain [people's] sympathy, or at the very least neutralize them' (2006, p. 52). In other words, media should play three functions including persuading a large number of people to join the jihad, 'offer[ing] positive support, and adopt[ing] a negative attitude toward those who do not join the ranks' (pp. 50–51). Media should also address people living outside the group's control to instigate them 'to fly to the regions which we manage, particularly the youth after news of (our) transparency and truthfulness reaches them so that they may be fully aware of the loss of money, people, and worldly gains' (p. 51). The last group that needs to be targeted includes enemy combatants particularly 'who have lower salaries, in order to push them to join the ranks of the mujtahids or at least to flee from the service of the enemy' (pp. 50–51).

Several audiovisual materials released by ISIS stress the importance of media in supporting the Islamic State in line with Naji's above recommendations. In one example, the Shumukh Instigation Workshop (n.d.) released a video entitled 'Journalist, you're a Jihadist' in which several interviews with ISIS fighters were conducted. Many responded on the role of media, stating: 'Your support lifts the morale of ISIS fighters'. The video's goal is to provide a social media literacy crash course on whom to follow, block, and how to retweet as well as the importance of protecting one's online privacy by using the Dark Web (Tor network) and virtual private networks (VPNs). In several selected examples, the narrator provides the following online advice: 'You need to group all links in a file sharing site; publish the link in the body of the tweet and fill the rest with hashtags'. Indeed, the primary message in this training video is 'Your tweets are your weapons', and that those who tweet for ISIS are also 'mujahedeen just like those who are fighting in the field' (Shumukh Instigation Workshop, n.d.). Other ISIS efforts to educate its followers on the use of Twitter have come from Afaaq Electronic Foundation, which is specifically focused on 'raising security and technical awareness' among jihadists (O'Neill, 2016).

Another important printed Arabic work that was released by ISIS is entitled *Journalist, you're a Mujahid* (ISIS, 2015). The booklet begins with a quotation by Osama Bin Laden on the importance of media role in jihad, stating:

> Journalists and writers have a great and significant impact in directing the battle, demoralizing the enemy, and lifting up the nation's morale… It is the time now for media to take its right place and perform its required role in countering the fierce campaign and public crusading war [against Islam]. This must be done in all media forms: visual, audio, and written. Media workers, whether be journalists, analysts, or correspondents, must be up to the level of responsibility and the [gravity of] events in performing their required role, enlightening the

> nation, and showing the reality of the enemies by revealing their plans and schemes. They should all stand up in one front with all their affiliations as the enemy today does not differentiate between one group or another.
>
> (ISIS, 2015, p. 10)

The booklet details various aspects of media work that can assist ISIS in its mission, for media is regarded as 'a double-edged sword as it can please the faithful and make the enemies agitated' (ISIS, 2015, pp. 33–34). In its vision of a media system, journalists have a vital role in countering a cultural invasion 'that is more powerful than a military one' (p. 44), while an emphasis is placed on creating a totalitarian structure wherein 'the journalist must obey the order of his Emir or his media superior who has assigned tasks and duties and [often] prefers that the journalist works in a certain region' (p. 36).

In addition, various audio and visual productions were produced by an 'army of journalists' who should never complain for working long hours because they are part of jihad and 'will be rewarded with a promise to enter Heaven' (ISIS, 2015, pp. 20–21). In other words, journalists are 'regarded as jihadists similar to other ones' because they urge for jihad (p. 25), and they should perform their duties similarly to the way soldiers do in an army.

Interestingly, the booklet lists some principles of good journalism since 'monotheistic and faithful journalists [should] say the truth and express justice at a time when truth sayers are rare' (ISIS, 2015, p. 40). This official ISIS publication stresses the need to convey reality as it is

> at a time when most – if not all – of the well-known media outlets have professed in lying together with their journalists who have become experts in fabrication. They have accepted to become amplifiers of atheism, prostitution, and deceit and have combated religion and decency.
>
> (p. 42)

Again, it is crucial to reiterate that ISIS has run a very sophisticated and organized media body. As another example to this point, an ISIS correspondent nicknamed Abu Salih revealed to Iraqi authorities after being captured in 2016 that the terrorist group insisted on having a very centralized effort in running its media bureaus that were structured in a hierarchical system involving correspondents, copy editors, and graphic designers. The correspondents only took videos and pictures in high-definition quality to generate visual appeal for ISIS' messages. These items were then sent to ISIS' Amaq news agency, which ran detailed editorial reviews of all media materials to ensure their credibility before disseminating or archiving them. Each correspondent was responsible for a certain district or area in the Iraqi and Syrian provinces, whether under the control of ISIS or not (Al-Qudus Al-Arabi, 2016).

From a journalistic perspective, ISIS has attempted to give more credibility to its messages (Miller & Higham, 2015) and the Amaq News Agency, whose 'reporters try to appear objective' (Callimachi, 2016), carefully choose special terms to demonstrate some kind of transparency. Further, ISIS' systematic media strategies also included sophisticated digital recruitment and radicalization efforts through 'virtual coaches' that often employed encrypted mobile technologies and social media. For example, when ISIS wanted to recruit a member in India through Twitter, they asked him to use ChatSecure mobile app and then do the following:

> When he used his laptop, he was told to contact the handler via Pidgin, anotherencrypted tool. He was told to create an account with Tutanota, a secure email service. And the handler taught Mr. Yazdani how to use the Tails operating system, which is contained on a USB stick and allows a user to boot up a computer from the external device and use it without leaving a trace on the hard drive.
>
> (Callimachi, 2017)

In relation to online media, Arquilla and Ronfeldt (2001) introduced the concept of 'netwars' to describe the situation in which various groups seem to be small, dispersed, and often disorganized in what is termed as an 'internetted' practice. Indeed, this new sociotechnical reality defines the nature of the 'cyber army' of ISIS, and it increases the difficulty of curbing its online influence. ISIS uses only a few centralized Twitter accounts that 'tweet official statements and news updates' as well as provincial accounts run from the provinces ISIS controls 'which publish a live feed about [local] Isis operations' (Kingsley, 2014).[1] It is relevant to note here that many women are actively supportive of ISIS, which can be found in the example of the Al-Khanssaa Brigade and their online presence represented in spreading pro-ISIS messages especially due to their high connectivity (Manrique et al., 2016).

The centralization of ISIS' media division is further evident in the hierarchy of its leadership. As one example, in September 2016, the Pentagon announced that it killed Wael Adel Al-Fayadh, or Dr. Wael, who was regarded as ISIS' Minister of Information (BBC Arabic, 2016; Warrick, 2017). Al-Fayadh was responsible for supervising the production of promotional productions in the different provinces controlled by ISIS. He was also close to Mohammed Al- Adnani, the former spokesperson of ISIS, who was also killed in an earlier US drone attack. As of September 2023, the spokesperson of ISIS was Abu Huthaifa al-Ansari (NBC News, 2023).

Aside from the above activities, ISIS also supported hacking groups which could be regarded as part of its cyber army. For example, the Cyber Caliphate as well as the Hackers' Union of the Caliphate were one of ISIS' tools to exert influence as it often boasted of any successful attempts at hacking websites or social media outlets by using a network of sympathetic hackers from different parts of the world (BBC News, 2015). These efforts were sometimes organized and centralized, and there were reported to be approximately five hacking groups affiliated with ISIS that began working together in April 2016 under one banner called the 'United Cyber Caliphate' (Alkhouri, Kassirer, & Nixon, 2016; Al-Rawi, 2021). The efforts of these hacking groups also include blocking people or organizations on mobile apps and social media, such as the case of blocking 'Raqqa is slaughtered in Silence' on Telegram (Ashok, 2016), which is an encrypted mobile application. A theoretical framework on nation-states concept is offered in the following section.

Nation-State Building by ISIS

The envisioned jihadist nation-state represented ISIS' objective of creating a militant ideological entity. In the discourse on civil states, Benedict Anderson discusses the notion of states as 'imagined communities' that are often able to impose or create 'prime culture areas' (Postill, 2006, p. 16). Here, nations are in an imagined state because its members must continuously share a collective identity and think that they all belong to the same place. This is mostly done by the elites whose duty is to unify the members of the nation, and media plays an important role here. Anderson (2006) mentions how some South East Asian colonies were formed by making accommodation to and maintaining the impact of some religions like Islam and Buddhism as they 'could rarely do more than to regulate, constrict, count, standardize, and hierarchically subordinate these institutions to its own' (p. 169). In this regard, Geertz (1963) believes that the state needs to unify its people to better achieve its goals despite their ethnic, racial, and linguistic differences.

In this regard, the notions of state and an imagined jihadist nation-building are intertwined because ISIS intended to transform the nation into a militant state. Conceptually, 'nation' is a cultural term which is related to a group of people who have a number of binding features that provide them with a sense of commonality, while 'state' is a political term that refers to a group of people living in certain territories and following a number of rules and regulations dictated by those who hold power (Connor, 1978). The combination of the two terms is meant to indicate that 'politics and culture support each other, where a state derives the legitimacy to rule from its endorsement of a specific cultural group, and in turn a culture survives and thrives by the aid of political power' (Lu & Liu, 2018, p. 111).

In his seminal study on nation-building, Karl Deutsch (1963) argues that several elements contribute to the formation of states, including establishing economic production means, trade, education, and mass communication especially by offering communicative spaces. Ernest Gellner (2008) focuses on other aspects in nation-state building like the importance of educational and linguistic homogeneity and standardization, but he suggests that the role of media cannot be overlooked here since it enhances values and creates co-cultural group or cultural area. In this regard, Mylonas (2012) defines nation-state building as 'the process through which governing elites make the boundaries of the state and the nation coincide; by employing three main policies: accommodation, assimilation, and exclusion. In relation to accommodation, it is a reference to 'the ruling elites' option to retain the non-core group in the state, but grant the group special minority rights' (p. xx). On the contrary, 'exclusion policies, such as ethnic deportations and mass killings, remain a part of the repertoire of state elites around the world', while assimilation is more related to cultural genocide (p. xxi) by the intentional removal and destruction of previous political, religious, and historical symbols.

In general, there are violent and nonviolent means of nation-state building; however, accommodation and assimilationist policies are often nonviolent, though the latter are often 'coercive' (Mylonas, 2012, p. 23). In order to build a nation-state, the elite group must implement certain policies often with the use of force in order to ensure that the new political system can work. Historically, Smith (1986) states that there are four types of nation-state formations: the Western, for example, European countries; the Immigrant, for example, United States, Canada, and Australia; the Ethnic, for example, Japan; and the Colonial, for example, many Arab and African countries that were formed due to colonial powers (pp. 241–42).

In this and the following chapters, I argue that ISIS followed standardized and systematic nation-state building policies similar to the above strategies. Despite its terroristic ideology, ISIS is an example of such an imagined jihadist nation-state which makes it unique among other terrorist groups because of its ambition to create a physical (and possibly an internationally recognized) space for its followers and controlled subjects. Unlike other Islamist terrorist groups, ISIS had a unique advantage of mass recruiting civil servants and officials mostly from Iraq and Syria who had prior experience in running secular states and practicing a variety of coercive and noncoercive strategies; for example, when Saddam Hussein invaded and annexed Kuwait in 1991, he removed the word 'state of Kuwait' from the Iraqi curriculum by replacing it with the term 'governorate' in his attempt to wipe it from the map. This was an example of cultural genocide. In the occupied Kuwait, the Iraqi Baath regime insisted on using the Iraqi curriculum as well as its currency. Thousands of crimes were committed such as looting, killing, rape, and destruction

(Amnesty International, 1990a, 1990b), and major efforts were made to impose the Iraqinazation policy including changing the names of streets and using a unified Iraqi national flag. An eye-witness account mentioned the details of this assimilation policy, stating the following:

> During the fifth week of the occupation the Iraqis distributed an instruction sheet that read: "any house that possesses Kuwaiti flags, pictures of the Emir, flyers, or guns, will be burned. Any attack on the Iraqi army from any house will result in the burning of all the houses surrounding it in 360 degrees.
>
> (Ghabra, 1991, p. 119)

Kuwaitis and expatriates were asked to report to work, while Iraqis were appointed in senior administration posts. As part of the standardization policy, everyone was given Iraqi ID cards, and 'all Kuwaitis were ordered to get new license plates or risk punishment' (Ghabra, 1991, p. 121). Most importantly, the official Iraqi TV channel became the national television, and huge street billboards were installed showcasing pictures of Saddam Hussein-15 to 25 feet long and 10 to 15 feet … like monuments all over the city, in front of every major installation, government building, and so on (p. 115).

Although Saddam Hussein's regime was secular and used pan-Arab rhetoric, the techniques and policies followed were similar to the way ISIS practiced cultural genocide and assimilation in the different cities it controlled. ISIS followed standardized and systematic nation-state building policies which were largely borrowed from the Baath's regime strategies especially in the way the latter implemented accommodation, assimilation, and exclusion policies. However, ISIS attempted to do this using its own radical version of Islam as a unifier, as will be later discussed. Most importantly, ISIS' elites purposefully tried to create a nation-state and collective identity with the use of media, yet this entity remained an imagined concept because its members 'will never know most of their fellow[s] … meet them, or even hear of them, yet in the minds of each lives the image of their communion'. This jihadist concept was only 'an imagined political community' (Anderson, 2006, p. 6).

Media and ISIS' Policies in Nation-State Building

Media and nation-state building are closely connected because media plays a highly important role in disseminating the idea of 'imagined communities' especially in enhancing the national identity of the nation's diverse and scattered members. Whether they are called 'communicative spaces' (Deutsch, 1963), 'cultural areas' (Gellner, 2008), or 'prime culture areas' (Postill, 2006), assimilation policies intend to shape a given culture through media in diverse ways. Here, media is used as a medium for achieving unity among people. Ross Poole (1999), for example, mentions that socialization, language, and mass media play important roles in forming the national identities of most individuals living in a certain nation (p. 14). Furthermore, John Postill (2006) discusses the third wave of nation building represented in Malaysia in 1963 and other South East Asian countries and emphasizes that the role of media is 'integral to their formation and maintenance' (p. 15). A.D. Smith (1989) mentions here that states are partly shaped by emphasizing a unique type of mythology and symbolism enhanced by mass communication and education to convince and influence the masses (p. 361), and one of the main elements that assist media and nation-state building in shaping national identities is, in fact, standardization. People living in a certain nation-state need to consume and absorb the same messages, symbols, and cultural practices to feel a sense of shared values, beliefs, and outlook toward life. In this regard, Stein Rokkan (1999) argues that there are four main institutional solutions in nation-state building such as standardization which incorporates 'conscript armies, compulsory schools, mass media, creating channels for direct contact between the central elite and parochial populations of the peripheries' (p. 83). As indicated above, standardization incorporates several aspects such as language, education, and media.[2]

As explained above, nation-state building requires a great deal of standardization as well as systematic efforts, and ISIS tried to achieve some of these goals with the assistance of former secular and civic officials from Iraq and elsewhere. In terms of accommodation, the terrorist organization was run by senior members or elites mostly consisting of former Iraqi intelligence officers (Coles & Parker, 2015). In its initial formation, Abu Bakr Al Baghdadi sought to bring in more former Baathists, especially those who had military and intelligence background (Tønnessen, 2015). Liz Sly (2015) lists a few shared ties that connect the Baathists with ISIS, such as the reliance of sophisticated intelligence networks, smuggling tactics to sell oil and avoiding sanctions, using fear to frighten the masses, branding themselves as transnational movements (pan-Arabism vs. pan-Islamism), and running camps for foreign fighters.

In nation-state building, elites are needed to manage the nation, and captured documents show that ISIS had a systematic hierarchy and bureaucracy in which the elites played important roles (Reuter, 2015); for example, 'society has seen the rise of a new elite class – the jihadi fighters – who enjoy special perks and favor in the courts, looking down on "the commoners" and even ignoring the rulings of their own clerics' (Hendawi, 2016). In this hierarchy, there were departments responsible for managing '"war spoils" including slaves, and the exploitation of natural resources such as oil, creating the trappings of government that enable it to manage large swaths of Syria and Iraq and other areas' (Landay, Strobel, & Stewart, 2015). This systematic management effort in nation-state building included diverse aspects like hiring specialized services for paving roads or cleaning streets, issuing ID cards, running schools, printing standard school curriculum that corresponded with ISIS' terrorist ideology, regulating trade, imposing taxes, setting sharia laws… and so on. 'Hundreds if not thousands of cadres have set themselves to work creating rules and regulations on everything …' (Malik, 2015). As a result, ISIS' imagined nation-state was formed based on social classes and coercive power enshrined by strict sharia laws similar to the way totalitarian secular states were run.

As for exclusion policies in nation-state building, they include ethnic cleansing and deportation of certain ethnic or religious groups. Here, Andreas Wimmer (2006) discusses the ethnic boundary enforcement in nation-state building which is related to the elite's institutionalized discrimination policy (p. 340), and ISIS was known to have practiced such a policy in the way Yazidi men were killed and their women were raped and enslaved, or in the mass killing of Shiite soldiers at Camp Speicher in Tikrit partly to enhance the sectarian tension between Shiites and Sunnis (Cockburn, 2015). At the same time, the properties of large numbers of Iraqi Christians living in Mosul and elsewhere were confiscated (Hawramy, 2014). In an ISIS document entitled 'The principles of administering the Islamic State', the general structure of the organization was revealed including its vision of a very divisive society. Instead of accepting minorities, the document mentioned the importance of removing the old school secular curriculum in Syria partly because it 'focused on … rejecting division among the sects which led to diminishing the Sunni identity' (Islamic State Blueprint, 2014).

Finally, and in relation to the assimilation policy in nation-state building which is related to cultural genocide, ISIS systemically tried to erase the secular roots of the Syrian and Iraqi societies by enhancing and planting a Salafist and militant interpretation of Islam in all aspects of life starting from what men and women should wear and up to the destruction of tombs and archeological sites. As for actual assimilation practices, special attention was devoted to children because ISIS wanted to plant the seeds of radicalization in them. In fact, ISIS called children 'Ashbal Al Khilafa' or the cubs of the Caliphate (RT, 2015) as part of introducing its own militarized vision of childhood, and it was estimated that about 50,000 children were living under ISIS' control in early 2016 (Townsend, 2016) who were compelled to attend school or their parents would be punished (CNN Arabic, 2015). In this regard, an ISIS document written in Arabic contained instructions directed to Syrian schools, instructing teachers and educators to get rid of all secular images from the curriculum that do not correspond with Islamic Sharia as well as removing the phrase 'the Arab Syrian republic' and the words 'home' or 'homeland' wherever they occurred by replacing them with the term 'Islamic State'. The document instructed the following: 'Do not teach the concept of [secular] nationalism and pan-Arabism but instead teach the idea of belonging to Islam and its followers' (Al Malah, 2015). Even mobile apps targeting children were designed to teach them standard Arabic language as well as ISIS' militant ideology (Knox, 2016).

To sum up, many nation-state building endeavors by ISIS were standardized, since they were observed in the different cities and regions (*willayat*) that the terrorist group controlled, requiring a collective effort. ISIS took advantage of the failed states of Iraq and Syria to recruit some former Baathists who, despite their original secular tendencies, had ample experience in running civil states. Besides, standardization gave some form of legitimacy to the group's militant brand and projected it as fearful establishment especially if continuous violence and intimidation were practiced. ISIS' general goal was to subdue the masses with fear tactics, erase the previous cultural and secular heritage and spaces, and cleanse the society from unwanted members. ISIS used its own hybrid version of Salafist Islam (Hassan, 2016), hoping to achieve its nation-building goals with the active use of jihadist propaganda.

Notes

1 It is important to mention that ISIS' fan clubs, sympathizers, and followers on social media largely operated without centralization (Melchior, 2014) or an 'obvious hierarchical structure', suggesting that online activity was largely 'driven by self-organization' (p. 1460). More discussion on Twitter is found in Chapter 2 of this book.

2 In relation to language, it has always been important in nation-state building as it is used as 'a salient identity symbol, as well as a political instrument' (Luong, 2004, p. 123). There are numerous examples on how language teaching and imposition has been used to unify the nation such as the case of enforcing Kazakh and Uzbek languages and vocabulary in Kazakhstan and Uzbekistan, particularly after the breakup of the Soviet Union (Ubiria, 2015) or the standardization of the Romani language of the stateless Roma people in the Baltic states (Daftary & Grin, 2003). Other examples of language standardization include Zimbabwe (Ndhlovu, 2009), Bosnia (Kolstø, 2016), and other part of Southeast Asia like Indonesia (Sercombe & Tupas, 2014). In relation to education, the standardization of the American educational system and curricula have been regarded as a crucial element in 'the development of national and state content and performance standards ... [which] are an instrument of public control of education' (Rapport, 2015, p.164). In other words, standardization provides an important centralized tool for the nation-state to control and monitor the overall educational process. Other aspects of standardization include laws such as the case of Turkey (Aslan, 2014, p. 146) and currency.

References

Ali Musawi, M. (2010, August). Cheering for Osama: How jihadists use Internet discussion forums. Quilliam. www.media-diversity.org/additional-files/cheering-for-osama.pdf

Alkhouri, L., Kassirer, A., & Nixon, A. (2016). Hacking for ISIS: The emergent cyber threat landscape. Flashpoint. https://iici.io/storage/media/2016/6/1014833787/files/474992437698232546.pdf

Al Malah, A. (2015, December 10). The complete story of ISIS curriculum in Caliphate land… Learn about it. *Arabi Post*. https://shorturl.at/prBJ2

Al-Qudus Al-Arabi. (2016, November 13). A journalist from the "Islamic State" organization reveals the secrets of the organization's media machine and the "professionalism" of field coverage. www.alquds.co.uk/?p=629253

Al-Rawi, A. (2016). Video games, terrorism, and ISIS's Jihad 3.0. *Terrorism and Political Violence*, *28*(4), 1–35. http://dx.doi.org/10.1080/09546553.2016.1207633

Al-Rawi, A. (2021). *Cyberwars in the Middle East*. Rutgers University Press.

Altheide, D. L. (2007). The mass media and terrorism. *Discourse & Communication*, *1*(3), 287–308. https://doi.org/10.1177/1750481307079207

Amnesty International. (1990a, December 19). *Iraq/occupied Kuwait human rights violations since 2 August 1990* [News Release]. AI index: MDE 14/16/90. www.amnesty.org/en/documents/mde14/016/1990/en/

Amnesty International. (1990b, October 3). *Iraqi forces killings and torturing in Kuwait, says Amnesty* [News Release]. AI Index: MDE 14/15/90.

Anderson, B. (2006). *Imagined communities: Reflections on the origin and spread of nationalism*. Verso Books.

Arquilla, J., & Ronfeldt, D. (2001). *Networks and netwars: The future of terror, crime, and militancy*. Rand Corporation.

Ashok, I. (2016, November 3). International Business Times. www.ibtimes.co.uk/pro-isis-hackers-claim-shutting-down-telegram-channel-raqqa-based-syrian-activist-group-1589635

Aslan, S. (2014). *Nation building in Turkey and Morocco*. Cambridge University Press.

Baudrillard, J., & Valentin, M. (2002). L'esprit du terrorisme. *The South Atlantic Quarterly*, *101*(2), 403–415. https://muse.jhu.edu/article/30752

BBC Arabic. (2016, September 16). Pentagon: The killing of a prominent ISIS leader in a raid near Raqqa in Syria. www.bbc.com/arabic/middleeast/2016/09/160916_syria_pentagon_isis_leader

BBC News. (2015, October 16). Malaysia arrests Kosovo man for 'hacking US files for IS.' www.bbc.com/news/world-asia-34546793

Bueno de Mesquita, E., & Dickson, E. S. (2007). The propaganda of the deed: Terrorism, counterterrorism, and mobilization. *American*

Journal of Political Science, *51*(2), 364–81. https://doi.org/10.1111/j.1540-5907.2007.00256.x

Callimachi, R. (2015, June 27). ISIS and the lonely young American. *New York Times*. www.nytimes.com/2015/06/28/world/americas/isis-online-recruiting-american.html?_r=0

Callimachi, R. (2016, January 14). A news agency with scoops directly from ISIS, and a veneer of objectivity. *New York Times*. http://nyti.ms/1lbIyHh

Callimachi, R. (2017, February 4). Not 'lone wolves' after all: How ISIS guides world's terror plots from afar. *The New York Times*. www.nytimes.com/2017/02/04/world/asia/isis-messaging-app-terror-plot.html?_r=0

CBS. (2014, June 16). U.N.: ISIS committing war crimes in Iraq. www.cbsnews.com/video/u-n-isis-committing-war-crimes-in-iraq/

Chan, K., Li, L., Diehl, S., & Terlutter, R. (2007). Consumers' response to offensive advertising: A cross cultural study. *International Marketing Review*, *24*(5), 606–28. https://doi.org/10.1108/02651330710828013

Chulov, M. (2014, December 11). ISIS: The inside story. *The Guardian*. www.theguardian.com/world/2014/dec/11/-sp-isis-the-inside-story?CMP=share_btn_tw

CNN Arabic. (2015, March 14). Daesh imposes compulsory education in Al Khair province, flogging teachers and forces them to clean streets. http://arabic.cnn.com/isis-syria-education-teachers-punishment

Cockburn, P. (2015, April 7). Isis mass graves: Iraqi forensic teams recover remains of 1,700 military cadets slaughtered by militants near Tikrit. *The Independent*. www.independent.co.uk/news/ world/middle-east/isis-mass-graves-iraqi-forensicteams-recover-remains-of-1700-military-cadetsslaughtered-by-10160883.html

Coles, I., & Parker, N. (2015, December 11). The Baathists: How Saddam's men help Islamic State rule. *Reuters*. www.reuters.com/investigates/special-report/mideast-crisis-iraq-islamicstate/#:~:text=The%20Baathists%20have%20strengthened%20the,35%20Iraqis%20who%20recently%20fled

Connor, W. (1978). A nation is a nation, is a state, is an ethnic group is a… . *Ethnic and Racial Studies*, *1*(4), 377–400. https://doi.org/10.1080/01419870.1978.9993240

Conway, M., & McInerney, L. (2008). Jihadi video and auto-radicalisation: Evidence from an exploratory YouTube study. In D. Ortiz-Arroyo, H. L. Larsen, D. D. Zeng, D. Hicks, & G. Wagner (Eds.), *Intelligence and security informatics* (pp. 108–18). Springer. https://doi.org/10.1007/978-3-540-89900-6_13

Cottee, S. (2015, March 2). Why it's so hard to stop ISIS propaganda. *The Atlantic*. www.theatlantic.com/international/archive/2015/03/why-its-so-hard-to-stop-isis-propaganda/386216/

Dabiq. (2015, August). The final statement of Abū Sinān an-Najdī (may Allah accept him), 11. https://web.archive.org/web/20180923130041/https://azelin.files.wordpress.com/2015/09/the-islamic-state-e2809cdc481biq-magazine-11e280b3.pdf

Daftary, F., & Grin, F. (Eds.) (2003). *Nation-building, ethnicity and language politics in transition countries (ECMI)*. Local Government and Public Service Reform Initiative/European Centre for Minority Issues. www.ecmi.de/fileadmin/redakteure/publications/pdf/ECMI-Vol-II.pdf

Dahl, D., Frankenberger, K. D., & Manchanda, R. V. (2003). Does it pay to shock? Reactions to shocking and nonshocking advertising content among university students. *Journal of Advertising Research*, *43*(3), 268–80. https://doi.org/10.1017/S0021849903030332

Dahlberg, L. (2007). The Internet, deliberative democracy, and power: Radicalizing the public sphere. *International Journal of Media & Cultural Politics*, *3*(1), 47–64. https://doi.org/10.1386/macp.3.1.47_1

Dens, N., De Pelsmacker, P., & Janssens, W. (2008). Exploring consumer reactions to incongruent mild disgust appeals. *Journal of Marketing Communications*, *14*(4), 249–69. https://doi.org/10.1080/13527260802141231

Deutsch, K. (1963). *Nation-building and national development: Some issues for political research*. Atherton.

Farwell, J. P. (2014). The media strategy of ISIS. *Survival*, *56*(6), 49–55. https://doi.org/10.1080/00396338.2014.985436

Freedman, D., & Thussu, D. K. (2012). Introduction: Dynamics of media and terrorism. In D. Freedman & D. K. Thussu (Eds.), *Media & terrorism: Global perspectives*. Sage. https://doi.org/10.4135/9781446288429

Garrison, A. H. (2004). Defining terrorism: Philosophy of the bomb, propaganda by deed and change through fear and violence. *Criminal Justice Studies*, *17*(3), 259–79. www.academia.edu/14271744/Defining_terrorism_philosophy_of_the_bomb_propaganda_by_deed_and_change_through_fear_and_violence

Geertz, C. (Ed.) (1963). *Old societies and new states: The quest for modernity in Asia and Africa*. Free Press of Glencoe.

Gellner, E. (2008). *Nations and nationalism*. Cornell University Press.

Ghabra, S. (1991). The Iraqi occupation of Kuwait: An eyewitness account. *Journal of Palestine Studies*, *20*(2), 112–25. www.jstor.org/stable/2537204

Hassan, H. (2016, June 13). *The sectarianism of the Islamic State: Ideological roots and political context*. Carnegie Endowment for International Peace. https://carnegieendowment.org/2016/06/13/sectarianism-of-islamic-state-ideological-roots-and-political-context-pub-63746

Hawramy, F. (2014, July 24). 'They are savages,' say Christians forced to flee Mosul by Isis. *The Guardian*. www.theguardian.com/world/2014/jul/24/iraqi-christians-mosul-isis-convert-islam-or-be-executed

Hendawi, H. (2016, January 18). Islamic State's double standards sow growing disillusion. *AP Magazine*. https://apnews.com/article/306189053ce1409a8f7c887cae7fbf7a

ISIS. (2015). *Journalist, you're a Mujahid* (2nd ed.). Al-Himmah Library.

Islamic State Blueprint. (2014). The principles of administering the Islamic State. www.scribd.com/document/292084330/Islamic-State-blueprint#

Jaffer, N. (2015, June 24). The secret world of ISIS brides: 'U dnt hav 2 pay 4 ANYTHING if u r wife of a martyr.' *The Guardian*. www.theguardian.com/world/2015/jun/24/isis-brides-secret-world-jihad-western-women-syria

James, H. (2015, March 11). Female recruits to ISIS: The recruiter's call. *Global News*. https://globalnews.ca/news/1876491/female-recruits-to-isis-the-recruiters-call/

Jones, T., Cunningham, P. H., & Gallagher, K. (2010). Violence in advertising. *Journal of Advertising, 39*(4), 11–36. www.jstor.org/stable/25780657

Kingsley, P. (2014, June 23). Who is behind ISIS's terrifying online propaganda operation? *The Guardian*. www.theguardian.com/world/2014/jun/23/who-behind-isis-propaganda-operation-iraq

Klausen, J. (2015). Tweeting the Jihad: Social media networks of Western foreign fighters in Syria and Iraq. *Studies in Conflict & Terrorism, 38*(1), 1–22. https://doi.org/10.1080/1057610X.2014.974948

Knox, P. (2016, May 11). Evil ISIS using new smart phone app to brainwash kids into becoming jihadi killers. *The Daily Star*. www.dailystar.co.uk/news/latest-news/isis-islamic-state-cubs-caliphate-20686404

Kolstø, P. (2016). *Strategies of symbolic nation-building in South Eastern Europe*. Routledge.

Landay, J., Strobel, W., & Stewart, P. (2015, December 28). Exclusive: Seized documents reveal Islamic State's Department of 'War Spoils.' *Reuters*. www.reuters.com/article/ us-usa-islamic-state-documents-group-exc-idUSKBN0UB0AW20151228

Lu, J., & Liu, X. (2018). The nation-state in the digital age: A contextual analysis in 33 countries. *International Journal of Communication, 12*, 110–30. https://ijoc.org/index.php/ijoc/article/view/7343

Luong, P. J. (2004). *The transformation of Central Asia: States and societies from Soviet rule to independence.* Cornell University Press.

Malik, S. (2015, December 7). The Isis papers: Behind "death cult" image lies a methodical bureaucracy. *The Guardian.* www.theguardian.com/world/2015/dec/07/isis-papers-guardian-syriairaq-bureaucracy

Manrique, P., Cao, Z., Gabriel, A., Horgan, J., Gill, P., Qi, H., ... & Johnson, N. F. (2016). Women's connectivity in extreme networks. *Science Advances, 2*(6), e1501742. www.science.org/doi/10.1126/sciadv.1501742

McCoy, O. (2017, August 18). Bitcoins for bombs. Council on Foreign Relations. www.cfr.org/blog/bitcoin-bombs

Melchior, J. (2014). ISIS tactics illustrate social media's new place in modern war. *TechCrunch.* http://techcrunch.com/2014/10/15/isis-tactics-illustrate-social- medias-new-place-in-modern-war

Miller, G., & Higham, S. (2015, May 8). In a propaganda war against ISIS, the U.S. tried to play by the enemy's rules. *The Washington Post.* www.washingtonpost.com/world/national-security/in-a-propaganda-war-us-tried-to-play-by-the-enemys-rules/2015/05/08/6eb6b732-e52f-11e4-81ea-0649268f729e_story.html

Mylonas, H. (2012). *The politics of nation-building: Making co-nationals, refugees, and minorities.* Cambridge University Press.

Nacos, B. L. (1994). *Terrorism and the media.* Columbia University Press.

Naji, A. B. (2006). The management of savagery: The most critical stage through which the Umma will pass (W. McCants, Trans.). John M. Olin Institute for Strategic Studies, Harvard University. www.academia.edu/24287794/Abu_bakr_naji_the_management_of_savagery_the_most_critical_stage_through_which_the_umma_will_pass

NBC News. (2023, August 3). ISIS says its leader was killed by militants in Syria and names successor. www.nbcnews.com/news/world/isis-leader-killed-syria-abu-al-hussein-al-husseini-al-qurayshi-rcna98020

Ndhlovu, F. (2009). *The politics of language and nation building in Zimbabwe.* Peter Lang.

Neer, T., & O'Toole, M. E. (2014). The violence of the Islamic State of Syria (ISIS): A behavioral perspective. *Violence and Gender, 1*(4), 145–56. https://doi.org/10.1089/vio.2014.0037

Nelson-Field, K., Riebe, E., & Newstead, K. (2013). The emotions that drive viral video. *Australasian Marketing Journal (AMJ), 21*(4), 205–11. https://psycnet.apa.org/doi/10.1016/j.ausmj.2013.07.003

O'Neill, P. H. (2016, February 2). How ISIS trains militants in online security. *The Daily Dot.* www.dailydot.com/layer8/isis-aef-nsa-snowden-video/

Paletz, D. L., & Schmid, A. P. (Eds.). (1992). *Terrorism and the media.* Sage.

Poole, R. (1999). *Nation and identity*. Routledge.
Postill, J. (2006). *Media and nation building: How the Iban became Malaysian*. Berghahn Books.
Prucha, N. (2011). Online territories of terror—Utilizing the Internet for Jihadist endeavours. *Jihadism Online*. www.researchgate.net/publication/298345468_Online_territories_of_terror_-_Utilizing_the_Internet_for_jihadist_endeavors
Rapport, A. (2015). Facing the challenge: Obstacles to global and global citizenship education in US schools. In J. Zajda (Ed.), *Nation-building and history education in a global culture* (pp. 155–70). Springer. https://doi.org/10.1007/978-94-017-9729-0_10
Reuter, C. (2015, April 18). The terror strategist: Secret files reveal the structure of Islamic State. Spiegel International. www.spiegel.de/international/world/islamic-state-files-show-structure-of-islamist-terror-group-a-1029274.html
Rokkan, S. (1999). *State formation, nation-building, and mass politics in Europe: The theory of Stein Rokkan: Based on his collected works*. Clarendon Press.
RT. (2015, March 29). Caliphate's cubs conduct mass execution for the first time. https://shorturl.at/emLZ2
Schmid, A. (2005). Terrorism as psychological warfare. *Democracy and Security*, *1*(2), 137–46. www.jstor.org/stable/48602562
Schmid, A. P., & De Graaf, J. (1982). *Violence as communication: Insurgent terrorism and the western news media*. Sage.
Seib, P., & Janbek, D. M. (2011). *Global terrorism and new media: The post-Al Qaeda generation*. Routledge.
Sercombe, P., & Tupas, R. (Eds.) (2014). *Language, education and nation-building: Assimilation and shift in Southeast Asia*. Springer.
Shumukh Instigation Workshop. (n.d.). Journalist, you're a Jihadist. https://archive.org/details/OhMediaCorrespondent...YouAreAMujahid [Link active as of January 5, 2016]
Siemaszko, C. (2014, July 13). U.S. Jihadis being recruited by ISIS via Skype to attack overseas—or at home. *New York Daily News*. www.nydailynews.com/news/crime/u-s-jihadis-recruited-isis-skype-article-1.1854216
Sly, L. (2015, April 4). The hidden hand behind the Islamic State militants? Saddam Hussein's. *The Washington Post*. www.washingtonpost.com/world/middle_east/the-hidden-hand-behind-the-islamic-state-militants-saddam-husseins/2015/04/04/aa97676c-cc32-11e4-8730-4f473416e759_story.html
Smith, A. D. (1986). State-making and nation-building. In J. A. Hall (Ed.), *States in history* (pp. 228–63). Blackwell.

Smith, A. D. (1989). The origins of nations. *Ethnic and Racial Studies, 12*, 340–67. https://doi.org/10.1080/01419870.1989.9993639

Smith, J. (2015, March 7). ISIS and Twitter. *The Guardian.* http://guardianlv.com/2015/03/isisand-twitter/

Spencer, R. (2014, June 16). Iraq crisis: UN condemns 'war crimes' as another town falls to Isis. *The Guardian.* www.telegraph.co.uk/news/worldnews/middleeast/iraq/10904414/Iraq-crisis-UN-condemns-war-crimes-as-another-town-falls-to-Isis.html

Stern, J., & Berger, J. M. (2015). *ISIS: The state of terror.* HarperCollins.

Szoldra, Paul. (2015). Here's how the military tracked down and killed the top hacker for ISIS. Tech Insider. www.businessinsider.com/isis-hacker-trick-found-2016-6

Tait, R. (2014, June 14). ISIS' half-a-billion-dollar bank heist makes it world's richest terror group. *The Telegraph.* www.telegraph.co.uk/news/worldnews/middleeast/iraq/10899995/ISIS-half-a-billion-dollar-bank-heist-makes-it-worlds-richest-terror-group.html

Tønnessen, T. H. (2015). Heirs of Zarqawi or Saddam? The relationship between al-Qaida in Iraq and the Islamic State. *Perspectives on Terrorism, 9*(4), 48–60. www.ffi.no/en/publications-archive/heirs-of-zarqawi-or-saddam-the-relationship-between-al-qaida-in-iraq-and-the-islamic-state

Townsend, M. (2016, March 5). How Islamic State is training child killers in doctrine of hate. *The Guardian.* www.theguardian.com/world/2016/mar/05/islamic-state-trains-purer-child-killers-in-doctrine-of-hate

Ubiria, G. (2015). *Soviet nation-building in Central Asia: The making of the Kazakh and Uzbek Nations.* Routledge.

Venhaus, J. (2010, May). *Why youth join Al-Qaeda.* United States Institute of Peace. www.usip.org/sites/default/files/resources/SR236Venhaus.pdf

Warrick, J. (2017, August 18). ISIS's propaganda machine is thriving as the physical caliphate fades. *The Washington Post.* www.washingtonpost.com/world/national-security/isiss-propaganda-machine-is-thriving-as-the-physical-caliphate-fades/2017/08/18/4808a9f6-8451-11e7-ab27-1a21a8e006ab_story.html?utm_term=.39156f2d9196

Weimann, G. (2005). The theater of terror: The psychology of terrorism and the mass media. *Journal of Aggression, Maltreatment & Trauma, 9*(3–4), 379–90. https://doi.org/10.1300/J146v09n03_08

Wilkinson, P. (1997). The media and terrorism: A reassessment. *Terrorism and Political Violence, 9*(2), 51–64. https://doi.org/10.1080/09546559708427402

Wimmer, A. (2006). Ethnic exclusion in nationalizing states. In G. Delanty & K. Kumar (Eds.), *The Sage handbook of nations and nationalism* (pp. 334–44). Sage. https://doi.org/10.4135/9781848608061

Wright, J. (1991). *Terrorist propaganda: The red army faction and the provisional IRA, 1968–86.* Macmillan.

Wright, L. (2006, Sep. 11). The master plan: For the new theorists of jihad, Al Qaeda is just the beginning. *The New Yorker*. www.newyorker.com/magazine/2006/09/11/the-master-plan?currentPage=all

1 Billboards*

Introduction

This chapter deals with the Islamic State of Iraq and Syria (ISIS) and its nation-state building efforts with the assistance of media productions such as billboards. This chapter is focused on some productions released by Al-Himmah Library which is ISIS' official printing press. ISIS sought to create a jihadist nation-state whose ideology is focused on imposing a strict version of sharia law, conducting ongoing religious wars, and restoring old Islamic empires. In order to achieve this goal, ISIS used media as a means because it is regarded as an important tool in mobilizing the public and gathering support.

For ISIS, media is considered as a form of jihad and journalists are jihadists whose roles are as important as those who use arms. In the following section, a discussion is presented on the way ISIS used standardized media methods and productions in order to promote the idea that it was a unified nation-state entity rather than a fake one.

ISIS' Standardized Media Productions

ISIS used many offline communication techniques in an attempt to influence people who lived under its control as part of the terrorist group's jihadist nation-state building efforts. In relation to the

* This chapter is largely based on a previous study whose details are as follows: Al-Rawi, A. (2019). Islamic State in Iraq and Syria's standardized media and jihadist nation-state building efforts. *Communication and the Public*. 1–15.

DOI: 10.4324/9781032615882-2

manner of dissemination, books and pamphlets were distributed by hand to as many people as possible since face-to-face dissemination and offline communication activities were regarded as standard practices followed in the different regions under ISIS control (see Figure 1.1). These communication techniques were similar to that followed by ISIS' Al-Husba religious police which was responsible for imposing ISIS' strict religious rules in relation to clothing and behavior.

All of the offline promotional items were posted online in various printable layouts; for example, almost every publication was posted in different file formats, such as PDF and Bitmap, as well as in colored and black and white versions, which was meant to be printed in standardized ways in the different cities and regions under ISIS control. Since these publications were easily circulated online, they enhanced ISIS' efforts in consolidating its nation-state building activities as geographically diverse; ISIS-controlled

Figure 1.1 ISIS members distribute pamphlets and books to ordinary people in different cities.

Note: ISIS' Al-Himmah Library images are assembled here by the author: (1) Eqirbatt (Syria), (2) Qaryateen (Syria), (3) Ramadi (Iraq), (4) Harawh (Libya), (5) Yarmuk Camp (Syria), and (6) Manbaj (Syria).

Source: archive.org.

territories were able to consume and print the same promotional materials without the need to physically interact. For instance, Figures 1.2–1.4 show how the same billboards were used in diverse and scattered cities often located in different countries like Libya, Iraq, and Syria. Indeed, all of these standardization efforts assisted in branding the terrorist group as transnational nation-state and projecting the imagined idea of its expanding powerful outreach.

This section discusses ISIS' pamphlets and billboards which were collected from a variety of online sources using several Arabic Google searches such as 'promotional flex' and 'promotional billboards'. The time period of posting these publications is not known, but I searched Google over a period of 4 months in early 2016. Due to the large blocking effort on Twitter, the terrorist group heavily used blogs (https://adkhilafah.wordpress.com, http://dawaahaq.blogspot.ca, or http://aladnnani.blogspot.ca), forums, and well-known websites like justpastit, archive.org (Smith, 2015), and dawaalhaq.com in order to disseminate its

Figure 1.2 The same billboard dealing with women's attire (niqab wearing) used in different ISIS-controlled cities.

Notes: ISIS' Al-Himmah Library images are assembled here by the author: (1) Talafar (Iraq), (2) Mosul (Iraq), and (3) Sirt (Libya). The billboard lists seven conditions on the niqab's features such as being odorless in order not to attract attention.

Source: archive.org.

Figure 1.3 The same billboard calling for Jihad used in two different ISIS-controlled cities.

Notes: ISIS' Al-Himmah Library images are assembled here by the author: (1) Sirt (Libya) and (2) Raqqah (Syria). Citing the Wahabbi preacher, Ibn Taymiyyah, the billboard references the worldly and heavenly rewards of jihad.

Source: archive.org.

Figure 1.4 The same billboard promoting the group's alleged future victories used in three different ISIS-controlled cities.

Notes: ISIS' Al-Himmah Library images are assembled here by the author: (1) Talafar (Iraq), (2) Mosul (Iraq), and (3) Tikrit (Iraq). The billboard reads as follows: 'We'll be victorious despite the global crusading coalition'.

Source: archive.org.

various materials. One of the main data sources in this study was ISIS' publishing agency known as Al-Himmah Library (http://himmah1437.blogspot. ca), which ran an educational app targeting children and published hundreds of books, pamphlets, and wall posters. On this blog, 62 billboards, 56 pamphlets, 8 wall posters, and 19 books including school textbooks were posted. All the pamphlets (n = 70) and billboards (n = 77) mostly taken from the website above were examined in this study because they offered an important insight into ISIS' offline standardized media productions which remain largely under-researched. I am not aware whether the number of collected pamphlets and billboards is exhaustive due to the difficulty of conducting field research, and this remains one of the study's limitations.

Methodologically, I used thematic analysis (TA) to identify the main themes found in the examined offline publications by analyzing the texts and images. TA is a qualitative method based on grounded theory (Guest, MacQueen, & Namey, 2011) and uses inductive coding in what Wimmer and Dominick refer to as 'emergent coding'. Here, constructs are classified 'based on common factors or themes that emerge from the data themselves' (Wimmer & Dominick, 2013, p. 168). Themes are identified by observing patterns, commonalities, and repetitions in the messages that are textually and visually communicated (Strauss & Corbin, 1998; Guest et al., 2011). Finally, ISIS' offline publications are connected to the broader context since leaving 'a text analysis at the level of topics, explanatory themes, or frames runs the risk of accepting content in a one-dimensional way … while missing the complicated ideological context at play' (Fursich, 2009, p. 248).

In general, these offline publications focused on nine main themes revolving around imposing Islamic jurisdiction following the group's strict interpretation of Islam. The main highlighted themes and their frequencies in these offline publications are as follows:

1 Call for jihad (n = 32)
2 Women's garment appearance and behavior (n = 12)
3 Observing ISIS' sharia law (n = 73)
4 Men's garment appearance and behavior (n = 9)
5 Promoting ISIS as a functional state (n = 12)
6 Critical of Arab regimes (n = 2)

7 Critical of coalition forces ($n = 1$)
8 Antismoking ($n = 4$)
9 Call for using a new currency ($n = 2$).

As can be seen, the most prominent theme is observing Sharia law followed by calls for jihad, indicating the importance given by ISIS to these two issues. As an example of theme 3, one of the pamphlets provides 20 different reasons to remove satellite dishes and break them, while another one explains that loyalty should be for Islam rather than to one's secular homeland. Regarding themes 6 and 7, a few publications criticized Arab governments like Iraq, Syria, and Egypt as well as coalition forces for their military support or direct involvement against ISIS. As for theme 9, ISIS introduced and promoted a new currency called the golden dinar to replace national and foreign currencies. The dinar is similar to the currency used during the climax of the Muslim empire and control during the Abbasside period which was expected to offer a standardized currency that can provide authority and legitimacy to the Islamic state in the different territories it controlled.

As mentioned in the Introduction of this book, nation-state building is undertaken in several ways including accommodation, exclusion, and assimilation, and ISIS used offline publications as part of its jihadist nation-state building efforts and to brand itself as a real nation-state that could provide public services and protection for its subjects. For instance, there are a few anti-smoking publications which were meant to project the image of a nation-state concerned about the general health of its citizens using religious teachings, while others highlighted the alleged urban improvements that occurred in some cities such as Mosul. One prominent type of publications is that that calls for jihad (theme 1) with a clear message that targets men rather than women. There is an emphasis on the alleged 'heavenly rewards' for military relocation and remote stationing on the Islamic State's borders (Murabbatta) in order to encourage people to protect ISIS' territory. Men's garment and appearance are also highlighted in some of these publications, with a special focus on their long beards, shaved mustaches, and short gowns. However, many productions target women, especially those that highlight the importance of their garments, for example, niqab wearing (see Figure 1.5). They provide detailed instructions on the 'proper' way of dressing in

Figure 1.5 Billboards instructing women on how to wear their garments (niqab).

Note: Most of the above images are produced by ISIS' Al-Himmah Library and are assembled here by the author.

Source: archive.org.

full women's clothing, including the niqab. One of the billboards shows an empty throne, while the text reads: 'The Muslim woman is a Queen at her house', with a Quranic verse 'Stay at your homes' (Al-Ahzab – 33). Human Rights Watch (2016) conducted interviews with 21 Sunni Arab women who lived under ISIS' control, and the report stated the following in relation to the assimilation policies of ISIS:

> All women … reported being forced to wear the niqab, which covers body, face, and head, with veils over their eyes, gloves, and socks whenever they left their houses. All clothing had to be black and without decoration. Many said that with their eyes veiled, they could not see where they were going and

> sometimes stumbled and fell. Before ISIS took over their areas, they said, they wore headscarves with their faces showing, and colored clothing.

In this regard, women were compelled to convert to ISIS' ideology, or they risked being harshly punished. ISIS' Al-Khanssaa Brigade, for example, consisted only of women, who released a manifesto in 2015 in which the group emphasized 'the importance of motherhood and family support'. The publication itself is 'fundamentally misogynist and, within its interpretation of Islamism, the role of women is "divinely limited"' (Winter, 2015a, p. 5). Indeed, the teachings of this manifesto could be clearly observed in these billboards that target women.

In terms of assimilation, which is related to cultural genocide, ISIS imposed its strict Islamic rules by force, and any offenders were harshly punished by the Husba police. In this regard, all billboards assisted ISIS in its nation-state building efforts by their call for adopting a new non-secular way of living. To give the messages some legitimacy, most of the publications, if not all, contain Quranic verses or some of Prophet Muhammed's sayings. As for publications dealing with sharia law, the terrorist group planned on managing an imagined nation-state allegedly similar to what appeared in early Islam (Shane & Hubbard, 2014; Thielman, 2014), particularly in connection to religious rules, duties and obligations (Winter, 2015b) such as almsgiving and praying on time. All the sharia-promoting publications are meant to brand ISIS as a purely Islamic group, so an attack against it is communicated to its followers as an attack against Islam itself. Other publications that urge for jihad include persuasive messages that present the terrorist group as a defender of Muslims, while jihad is meant to protect Islam and Sunni Muslims in general. In fact, ISIS repeatedly portrays itself as 'the protective vanguard for the world's Sunni Muslims' (Cottee, 2015; Quilliam, 2014, p. 32) which can be regarded as an important appeal and recruiting factor for jihad. To better understand ISIS' standardized media and nation-state building efforts, a brief concluding discussion is provided on the terrorist group's media strategy in the following section.

As an example of assimilation, many streets' billboards discussed here show the constant obsession ISIS had with imposing its strict sharia laws and teachings on all people since it was fiercely trying to indoctrinate the society by spreading its messages and militarizing it. Based on several direct eyewitness accounts from ISIS' previously controlled regions, the terrorist group normally lashed people who were viewed as offenders or violators of their own Islamic rules, such as listening to music or allowing women to leave their homes without a male companion, and 'if someone doesn't believe they cut his ear' (Speckhard & Yayla, 2015, p. 114). For more serious offenses like homosexuality or fornication, ISIS normally resorted to killing.

Regarding it as part of its fights against its enemies, ISIS placed great importance on media in relation to its nation-state building activities. In terms of standardized policy, ISIS was paranoid when it came to private and uncensored Internet networks as well as satellite dishes which were both banned in its controlled territories (Ali, 2016; Coles & Parker, 2015; Malik, 2015). Internal ISIS documents show that this ban extended to print publications especially that the group burnt several libraries in order to limit what people can read. For example, some of ISIS' documents mention that it is absolutely forbidden to circulate any publications, newspapers, or educational schedules not issued by the Islamic State offices in Wilayat Dimashq. And all books, newspapers, and stored newspapers will be confiscated in the offices and held by the Diwan al-Ta'aleem so as not to spread them (Zelin, 2015).

In order to organize these standardized laws, ISIS created a centralized media division similar to a Ministry of Information running several other media production centers like Al-Hayat, Al-Furqan, and Al-Ethar. Each province or city controlled by ISIS had a media department which disseminated materials in coordination with the military and security administrators (Islamic State Blueprint, 2014). In each city, there was also what is termed as 'Media Point' where people could receive ISIS' publications and forcibly watch its promotional videos. ISIS' media division had its own news agency called Amaq (depths) which ran its own Android app, and there was also *Al-Nabaa* newspaper, the monthly *Dabiq* magazine in Arabic and English as well as Al Bayan radio station which aired in different ISIS-controlled areas (Callimachi, 2016; Shiloach, 2015b). This media vision is similar to that what is followed by totalitarian secular states including the former Baath regime in Iraq. For example, media is largely expected to mobilize the public and propagate for the state in Baathist Syria and Iraq during Saddam Hussein's rule, Sudan, and Libya during Muammar Qaddafi's rule (Al-Rawi, 2012; Ayish, 2002; Rugh, 2004, pp. 29–31). Similar to ISIS' media policy, Saddam Hussein ran a Ministry of Information that oversaw and managed media production and a centralized Iraqi News Agency (INA) (Boyd, 1982).

In relation to social media, the terrorist group used only a few centralized Twitter accounts (Al-Rawi & Groshek, 2019) that 'tweet official statements and news updates' as well as provincial accounts run from the provinces that ISIS controls 'which publish a live feed about [local] ISIS operations' (Kingsley, 2014). The centralization of media messages was meant to standardize the message which was part of the nation-state building effort and branding a unified official image. This standardization was even seen in the kind of standard emojis ISIS followers often used (Shiloach, 2015a).

One of the earliest publications that is attributed to shaping the ideological foundations of ISIS is called 'The Management of Savagery' written by a jihadist called Abu Bakr Naji (2006) (Al-Rawi, 2018). In relation to media's role, Naji discusses how the media plays an important part in projecting the idea of a powerful nation-state which was what ISIS was obsessed with. He further stresses that the masses have to be persuaded, stating that the 'role of media politics is to gain [people's] sympathy, or at the very least neutralize them' (Naji, 2006, p. 52). In other words, media is viewed by ISIS as a propaganda tool that is used to directly influence people or to the very least silence them in order to be subdued. Specifically, media has three separate roles in relation to the masses living under the Islamic State's control, which include persuading 'a large number of them to join the jihad, offer[ing] positive support, and adopt[ing] a negative attitude toward those who do not join the ranks' (Naji, 2006, pp. 50–51). As for people living outside the group's control, media should also target them in order to 'motivate' them 'to fly to the regions which we manage, particularly the youth after news of (our) transparency and truthfulness reaches them so that they may be fully aware of the loss of money, people, and worldly gains' (Naji, 2006, p. 51). The last target group includes enemy combatants especially those 'who have lower salaries, in order to push them to join the ranks of the mujahids or at least to flee from the service of the enemy' (pp. 50–51). Due to its important role in jihad, Naji emphasizes the significance of creating a special media division which is what ISIS actually operated 'whose purpose is to communicate what we want to say to the masses and focus their attention on it, even if this requires exposing the group to danger that is comparable to the danger of a military operation …' (Naji, 2006, pp. 95–96). Indeed, Naji defines the jihadist struggles as 'media battles' (Naji, 2006, p. 73) waged against the 'infidels'.

In another important Arabic book publication entitled *Journalist, You're a Jihadist* that was distributed internally and posted online, we find a more elaborate vision of media's standardized role (Shumukh Instigation Workshop, n.d.).[1] The book begins by explaining that journalism is jihad and journalists are themselves jihadists because 'jihadist media has a great heavenly reward' (p. 10). The authors inquire the following: 'Have you not seen how the film maker carries his camera instead of the Kalashnikov and runs in front of the soldiers during the raids, receiving the bullets in his chest!' (p. 18). This militant vision of journalism is also found in a few other images released by ISIS on the role of media in the battlefield. In its insight on jihadist media, the authors stress that 'a journalist is a suicide attacker without a [suicide] belt' (p. 18).

In general, there is a clear importance given to media workers due to 'the gravity of their job' as well as their 'large responsibility' (p. 10). The book also emphasizes that 'the power of words is sometimes stronger than that of nuclear bombs' (p. 11), especially that media efforts complement military actions in the sense that media should aim at 'achieving psychological defeat of the enemy' since jihadist media is 'half the battle' (p. 11). The stated goal of the book is to 'prepare a new generation of media workers that are of high quality similar to the high standards that the Islamic State requires from its followers' (p. 11). In this regard, journalists' duties include writing articles, going to the battlefield (jihad with the self), urging for jihad, agitating the enemy, pleasing the faithful ones (ISIS followers), following the rulers' orders, covering reality, and countering cultural invasion. The publication insists that most if not all media outlets disseminate lies, while the role of ISIS' journalists is to be different by 'conveying to simple people the true picture of the battle without exaggeration or deception' (p. 40). However, ISIS' book itself clearly preaches the importance of media mobilization in which objectivity and neutrality can never be attained in ISIS' imagined jihadist nation-state. Also, unfavorable ISIS footage is never disseminated to the public (see, e.g., Vice News, 2016).

Several other audiovisual materials released by ISIS stress the importance of media in supporting the Islamic State. To give one example, Shumukh Instigation Workshop (n.d.) released a video with the title *Journalist, you're a Jihadist* in which several interviews with ISIS fighters were conducted. Many responded on the role of media, stating the following: 'Your support lifts the morale of ISIS fighters'. The video's goal is to provide a standardized social media literacy crash course on whom to follow, block, and how to retweet as well as the importance of protecting one's online privacy using the Dark Web (Tor network) and Virtual Private Networks (VPNs). The main message in this video is 'Your tweets are your weapons'. In brief, all of the above media goals are limited to mobilization and advocacy because they are meant to assist in the nation-state building efforts of ISIS in order to better achieve its intended objectives of creating a jihadist nation-state. This media vision is similar to that followed by totalitarian states as media is largely expected to mobilize the public and propagate for the survival of the state. This standardized media strategy is reminiscent of that which the former Baath regime in Iraq followed. For example, one of the most famous statements by Saddam Hussein was the following: 'The pen and rifle have one barrel' which was written on hundreds of thousands of school textbooks, buildings, and posters.

To sum up, ISIS intended to build a jihadist nation-state with the direct and indirect assistance of media due to its importance in disseminating pro-ISIS messages. Its goal was to indoctrinate people to actively participate in jihad and blindly follow all of its rules without questioning their superiors. As part of ISIS' efforts, standardized offline communication techniques were heavily used to target people living under ISIS' control, and most billboards and pamphlets focused on highlighting the importance of sharia law, calls for jihad, and marketing for the terrorists. Since the exact same offline media productions were found in different ISIS-controlled cities, they helped in providing a false impression of the group's imagined outreach. With its use of standardized messages as well as centralized media strategy and production departments,

ISIS attempted to create a stronger brand image whether be inside its territories or outside them. All of these efforts were meant to enhance the idea that ISIS created a real nation-state characterized by its jihadist ideology. With the defeat of ISIS in Iraq and most of Syria, the distribution of billboards, pamphlets, and textbooks became much more difficult offline, yet they continued circulating online, especially on the Dark Web and Telegram, as will be explained in Chapter 5. Other ISIS members and sympathizers used them for promotional and recruitment purposes because they served as a reminder of the terrorist group's once imagined jihadist nation-state.

Note

1 The Arabic word *Ellami* or media worker is translated as journalist here. It can also mean a media professional.

References

Ali, O. (2016, April 3). Daesh bans using satellite dishes in Mosul and tightens its grip on people. *Rudaw*. Retrieved from http://rudaw.net/arabic/middleeast/ iraq/030420161

Al-Rawi, A. (2012). *Media practice in Iraq*. Hampshire, UK: Palgrave Macmillan.

Al-Rawi, A. (2018). Video games, terrorism, and ISIS's Jihad 3.0. *Terrorism and Political Violence*, *30*, 740–60.

Al-Rawi, A., & Groshek, J. (2019). Jihadist propaganda on social media: An examination of ISIS related content on Twitter. *International Journal of Cyber Warfare and Terrorism*, *8*(4), 1–15.

Ayish, M. I. (2002). Political communication on Arab world television: Evolving patterns. *Political Communication*, *19*, 137–54.

Boyd, D. A. (1982). Radio and television in Iraq: The electronic media in a transitionary Arab world country. *Middle Eastern Studies*, *18*, 400–10.

Callimachi, R. (2016, January 14). A news agency with scoops directly from ISIS, and a veneer of objectivity. *The New York Times*. Retrieved from http://nyti.ms/1lbIyHh

Coles, I., & Parker, N. (2015, December 11). The Baathists: How Saddam's men help Islamic State rule. *Reuters*. Retrieved from www.reuters.com/investigates/ special-report/mideast-crisis-iraq-islamicstate/

Cottee, S. (2015, March 2). Why it's so hard to stop ISIS propaganda. *The Atlantic*. Retrieved from www.theatlantic.com/international/archive/2015/03/ why-its-so-hard-to-stop-isis-propaganda/386216/

Fursich, E. (2009). In defense of textual analysis. *Journalism Studies*, 10, 238–52.

Guest, G., MacQueen, K. M., & Namey, E. E. (2011). *Applied thematic analysis*. Thousand Oaks, CA: Sage.

Human Rights Watch. (2016, April 5). Iraq: Women suffer under ISIS. Retrieved from www.hrw.org/news/2016/04/05/iraq-women-suffer-under-isis

Islamic State Blueprint. (2014). The principles of administering the Islamic State. Retrieved from www. scribd.com/document/292084330/Islamic-Stateblueprint

Kingsley, P. (2014, June 23). Who is behind ISIS's terrifying online propaganda operation? *The Guardian*. Retrieved from www.theguardian.com/world/2014/jun/23/who-behind-isis-propagandaoperation-iraq

Malik, S. (2015, December 7). The Isis papers: Behind "death cult" image lies a methodical bureaucracy. *The Guardian*. Retrieved from www.theguardian. com/world/2015/dec/07/isis-papers-guardian-syriairaq-bureaucracy

Naji, A. B. (2006). *The management of savagery: The most critical stage through which the Umma will pass* (W. McCants, Trans.). Cambridge, MA: John M. Olin Institute for Strategic Studies, Harvard University.

Quilliam. (2014, December 19). Detailed analysis of Islamic State propaganda video: Although the disbelievers dislike it. Retrieved from www. quilliaminternational.com/shop/e-publications/detailedanalysis-of-islamic-state-propaganda-video-although-the-disbelievers-dislike-it/

Rugh, W. A. (2004). *Arab mass media: Newspapers, radio, and television in Arab politics*. New York, NY: Greenwood Publishing.

Shane, S., & Hubbard, B. (2014, August 30). ISIS displaying a deft command of varied media. *The New York Times*. Retrieved from www. nytimes.com/2014/08/31/world/middleeast/isis-displaying-a-deft-command-of-varied-media.html?partner=rss&emc=rss&smid=tw-nytimes&_r=0

Shiloach, G. (2015a, November 24). ISIS loyalists can download: A secret set of terrorist emojis. *Vocativ*. Retrieved from www.vocativ.com/254247/isis-loyalists-use-these-bloody-icons-like-emojis/

Shiloach, G. (2015b, November 30). This new ISIS app brings terror straight to your cell phone. *Vocativ*. Retrieved from www.vocativ.com/255768/this-new-isis-app-brings-terror-straight-to-your-cell-phone/

Shumukh Instigation Workshop. (n.d.). Journalist, you're a Jihadist. Retrieved from https://archive.org/details/OhMediaCorrespondent...YouAreAMujahid

Smith, J. (2015, March 7). ISIS and twitter. *The Guardian*. Retrieved from http://guardianlv.com/2015/03/isisand-twitter/

Speckhard, A., & Yayla, A. S. (2015). Eyewitness accounts from recent defectors from Islamic State: Why they joined, what they saw, why they quit. *Perspectives on Terrorism*, *9*, 95–118.

Strauss, A., & Corbin, J. (1998). *Basics of qualitative research: Techniques and procedures for developing grounded theory.* Thousand Oaks, CA: Sage.

Thielman, S. (2014, September 10). ISIS' sinister media strategy, and how the west is fighting back. *Adweek*. Retrieved from www.adweek.com/news/television/isiss-sinister-media-strategy-and-how-westfighting-back-160021

Vice News. (2016, April 27). What it's really like to fight for the Islamic State. Retrieved from https://news.vice.com/video/what-its-really-like-to-fight-for-the-islamic-state

Wimmer, R., & Dominick, J. (2013). *Mass media research: An introduction*. Boston, MA: Cengage Learning.

Winter, C. (2015a, February). Women of the Islamic State: A manifesto on women by the Al-Khanssaa Brigade. *Quilliam*. Retrieved from https://therinjfoundation.files.wordpress.com/2015/01/women-of-the-islamic-state3.pdf

Winter, C. (2015b, July). The virtual 'caliphate': Understanding Islamic State's propaganda strategy. *Quilliam*. Retrieved from www.stratcomcoe.org/download/file/fid/2589

Zelin, A. (2015, August 24). The archivist: 26 unseen Islamic State administrative documents: Overview, translation & analysis. *Jihadology*. Retrieved from http://jihadology.net/2015/08/24/the-archivist26-unseen-islamic-state-administrative-documentsoverview-translation-analysis/

2 Twitter*

Introduction

This chapter, which analyzes the efforts of the ISIS to promote itself and disseminate information on Twitter, examined a unique big data set on ISIS that included over 46 million tweets. Unlike most of the other chapters in this book that focus on the standardization and centralization of ISIS' media messages, this study examines jihadist propaganda by ISIS sympathizers and followers. The majority of previous studies focused on English language productions of ISIS, while this study empirically investigates Arabic language tweets, which further makes it a unique contribution to the literature on terrorists' groups branding on social media. The chapter also provides empirical evidence on the feud between Al-Qaeda and ISIS members, and how the latter members were pressuring other extremists to join ISIS through social media. Building on the theoretical concept of propaganda, the study discusses the way ISIS brands itself on Twitter in order to further understand how this terrorist group envisioned jihad and its objectives.

In this regard, there was a feud between Al-Qaeda and ISIS. Current Al-Qaeda leader Ayman al-Zawahiri disowned ISIS in 2013, leading to the creation of a jihadist global civil war especially

* This chapter is largely based on a previous study whose details are as follows: Al-Rawi, A. & Groshek, J. (2019). Jihadist propaganda on social media: An examination of ISIS related content on Twitter. *International Journal of Cyber Warfare and Terrorism*, *8*(4), 1–15.

DOI: 10.4324/9781032615882-3

after the declaration of the Caliphate by Abu Bakr Al-Baghdadi. al-Zawahiri justified his action by stating:

> We do not acknowledge this Caliphate. We do not see Abu Bakr al-Baghdadi as one worthy of the Caliphate... ..When Gaza was burning beneath Israeli bombs, Abu Bakr al-Baghdadi did not support it with one word, but his main concern was that all the mujahedeen pledge allegiance to him, after he assigned himself to be the Caliph without consulting them.
>
> (McConnell & Todd, 2015)

On its turn, nine former Al-Qaeda fighters joined ISIS and accused the group of committing different ‘unIslamic’ acts like ‘softness in dealing with the Shi’a, daring to declare that former Egyptian President Morsi was a Muslim, “excessive complimenting of what was called the Arab Spring”, supporting political work rather than fighting, and repudiating ISIS’ (Habeck, 2014). Due to the ideologically based feud, bloodshed followed between Al-Qaeda and ISIS ‘particularly after the Islamic State... demanded that Al Qaeda and all other Muslims obey its commands’ (McCants, 2016). This feud is evident in the social media data examined in this chapter, as will be explained below.

Here it is important to note that before being largely banned on Twitter, it was estimated that ISIS had about 46,000 Twitter accounts that were sympathetic or supportive of the group, most of which having been based in Iraq, Syria, and Saudi Arabia (Berger & Morgan, 2015, p. 2). In addition, the European Union commissioned the European Law Enforcement Agency, Europol, to block ISIS’ access to social media (BBC News, 2015). Of course, the decentralized nature of social media communication by ISIS sympathizers makes it challenging to counter ISIS messages (Melchior, 2014) even though social media itself can offer some potential security benefits such as disclosing valuable information about the location of some ISIS fighters (Castillo, 2015). According to Berger and Morgan’s study on ISIS Twitter accounts, 73% of followers selected Arabic as their main language followed by 18% English and 6% French, ‘a finding that tracks to some extent with the distribution of Western foreign fighters’ (2015, p. 14). In another related study, Milton (2016) examined 51 user accounts on Twitter that posted ISIS content and found that 'over 80 percent of them had been removed within two days of posting the Islamic State-related content' (p. 45).

Along these lines, several social media companies like Twitter, Facebook, and Google agreed to stop ISIS from freely disseminating its content on their platforms (Andrews & Seetharaman, 2016). From mid-2015 to early 2016, for example, Twitter shut down over 125,000 ISIS-linked accounts (Jeong, 2016). One study conducted by Milton (2016) showed that banning the group from social media has had some impact on the group's presence, and that its media production decreased considerably. Specifically, in August 2016, there were 194 posts from ISIS-linked media production units which were far fewer than the 761 posts found in August of the previous year before the censoring began. However, many observers believe that ISIS' sympathizers 'are everywhere on Twitter, despite the social-media network's efforts to ban them' (Cottee, 2015). In line with the above discussion, this chapter attempts to explore whether there are any ISIS followers who use popular references to the group on Twitter, namely ISIS and ISIL.

Based on this introduction and questions about the growth of ISIS during its peak years, particularly in recruiting outside core nations in the Middle East, this chapter seeks to better understand the online presence of ISIS on Twitter and investigate the nature of its members' interactions. The analysis was therefore guided by the following research question: In relation to its jihadist propaganda, was ISIS still active on Twitter? If yes, what did ISIS' followers tweet about?

In terms of method for this chapter, representative samples of tweets that mention the keywords 'ISIS' and 'ISIL' in English starting from October 2014 until early 2017 were drawn from the Boston University Twitter Collection and Analysis Toolkit (Borra & Rieder, 2014; Groshek, 2014).[1] As ISIS wanted people around the globe to use the term 'Islamic State in Iraq and the Levant' or 'Islamic State of Iraq and Syria' (الدولة الأسلامية في العراق والشام) in order to gain credibility among people since this description entails an acknowledgment that the terrorist group is both Islamic and a state, the two terms ISIS and ISIL were chosen to search for sympathizers who are more likely to use these mentions and hashtags. The average Muslims reject these two designations, preferring to call the terrorist group, Daesh. This is one of the reasons that explains why a large data set was analyzed that was collected from October 8, 2014 to February 12, 2017 and consisted of 50,412,848 tweets sent by 8,113,446 unique uses (28% of tweets contained no links). Hence, this study offers an analysis of one of the largest data sets that investigated ISIS on Twitter, and the frequency of tweets is summarized in Figure 2.1.

This period was chosen because it witnessed one of the most active periods during which ISIS became active online and offline. The reason behind choosing the English hashtag #ISIS is that it is a popular one that is often used by ISIS members inside and outside its controlled territories (Callimachi, 2017), since the Arabic acronym #DAESH (داعش) is regarded by the terrorist group as a derogatory one, as stated above. In the keyword searches, only Arabic language was used because it is considered the top language used by the majority of ISIS members (Berger & Morgan,

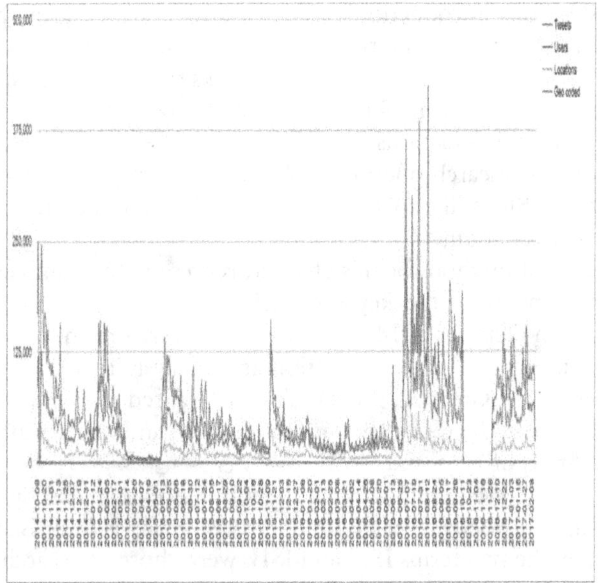

Figure 2.1 Frequency of 'ISIS' and 'ISIL' mentions on Twitter from October 8, 2014 to February 12, 2017.

Source: Author's creation.

2015) and that Arabic often accounts for '97% of all language uses' in ISIS-disseminated materials (Milton, 2016, p. 48).

In this first stage of the study, the intention was to examine whether the terrorist group is still actively present on Twitter by searching the data for sympathizers with the use of four Arabic keywords: staying (باقية), strengthened (تشتدد), Caliphate (خلافة), and Caliph (خليفة). These terms are often used by ISIS' sympathizers as their main mottos and goals to show that the group will remain united and strong (Al-Rawi, 2016). In the second stage of the study, the alleged feud between ISIS and Al- Qaeda terrorist groups is examined because it has not been empirically studied previously. For this purpose, we employed four Arabic keyword searches that are related to Al- Qaeda leaders: Laden (لادن), Al-Zawahiri (الظواهري), Al-Awlaki (العولقي), and Al-Zarqawi (الزرقاوي). Both stages of data analysis look at qualitative and quantitative markers of interactions to directly address the research question and make a contribution unique to terrorism research, and in studying ISIS.

In relation to the first stage of the study and to answer the research question, the results indicate that ISIS-related tweets – especially those that promote the group – dramatically decreased from late 2014 to late 2016 (see Figure 2.2). Four Arabic

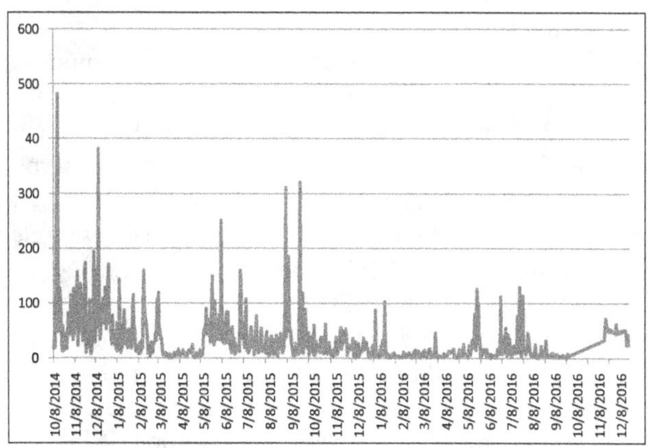

Figure 2.2 Frequency of tweets promoting ISIS.

Source: Author's creation.

Table 2.1 The most active Twitter users referencing pro-ISIS keywords

No.	*User*	*No. of tweets*
1	LinnOlsson16	1,619
2	ArmyYassin2	663
3	DrAhmadjoma	497
4	_Maqalat_	300
5	m5tsrj	204
6	boom9annboul	139
7	W2RISIS	129
8	booom9annnn	118
9	mr_ismail36	117
10	2550015_cr	111

language keywords were used and over 23,249 corresponding tweets were found which were sent by 11,728 unique Twitter users. Table 2.1 shows the most active pro-ISIS Twitter users who showed either direct or indirect sympathy or affiliation with the terrorist group. As of January 2017, all the users' accounts have been blocked except for one @DrAhmadjoma who often retweets and disseminates news on ISIS' expansions with a highly sectarian rhetoric. As of September 2023, this user is no longer on Twitter.

On another level of investigation and by using a computational method for text analytics, a program called WordStat was used to analyze 23,249 tweets in order to identify the most recurrent terms and phrases that assist in understanding the patterns and themes (Lopatin, Samuel-Azran, & Galily, 2017).

In relation to the thematic classification of these selected tweets, the insights drawn from this chapter reached results similar to that conducted by Milton (2016) and Klausen (2015) since the pro-ISIS tweets were mostly related to jihadist propaganda by promoting military achievements and reporting from battle, religious governance or instruction, interpersonal communication in the form of conversations among ISIS fighters, threats against the West and Islamic/Arab governments, and other posts that mention tourism or projecting a utopian view of ISIS-controlled lands. As shown in Table 2.2, the most recurrent phrases are principally related to boasting about the alleged victories of ISIS or threatening their enemies, while the Shiite-Sunni sectarian dimension is also evident. For example, one tweet in this list uses a pejorative term which is 'Shiites are donkeys' (n=252), while another refers to the 'Crusading and Safawi coalition'. The Safawi is a pejorative term for Shiites that invokes a historical association with the Persian invasion of some Arab lands in the 16th and 17th centuries. Most Shiite Arabs find the term derogatory against them (Mahood & Rane, 2017) partly because some Sunni extremists intentionally affiliate them with an ethnic Persian group that is distinct from other Shiites. What is prominent in all the phrases is that many of ISIS followers and sympathizers merely retweet the same message tens and sometimes hundreds of times by using different hashtags in order to spread the message as broad as they can to the social network.

By paying a closer examination of some ISIS Twitter users, we find that there is a clear coordination among them, which is part of interpersonal communication tweets mentioned above. For instance, the profile of @isis884 reads as 'Please do not follow me. The Islamic State remains'. One interpretation of this description is to attempt to remain anonymous or to hide the identity of other users in order to remain active online. Other Twitter users ask for coordination; for example, @allahmyloveme tweeted: 'Hey brothers, let's use an active hashtag to troll the infidels' (November 11, 2014), and some posts direct attacks on specific users. Examples of this practice include @HamzaHunter6 who called @ gaycaliph an 'apostate' (November 16, 2014), and @Abo3omar30 who requested his followers to 'support+follow+disseminate' five Twitter users who are also ISIS followers (January 11, 2015). The latter example is the most popular type of interpersonal communication tweets in these corpora, which aligns with previous studies. In one such example, in his study on ISIS on YouTube, Al-Rawi observed a similar online practice that was at least partially borrowed from the Swarmcast communication model (2016) where different ISIS users attempt to coordinate their efforts in order to support the group. In the study reported here, many users mention the Arabic hashtag 'Accounts that deserve support' (حسابات تستحق الدعم) in which they list a number of key ISIS members

Table 2.2 The top most recurrent phrases used in the tweets

No.	*Phrase*[a]	*Frequency*
1	باقيه وتتمدد [Remaining and expanding]	1,669
2	دولة الاسلام باقيه وتتمدد باءذن الله [The Islamic State remains and expands by Allah's willing]	1,619
3	ايها الكفار جئناكم بالخليفة الكرار دولتنا منصورة [Hey infidels, we've come to you with our courageous Caliph. Our State is victorious]	730
4	الشيعة حمير [Shiites are donkeys]	252
5	الخلافة ستكون واقعا [The Caliphate will be a reality]	225
6	النصيرية انتهت و تتبدد [The Nusairri (Syrian Alawite regime) has ended and disintegrated]	180
7	خوف الغرب من الخلافة الإسلامية [The Western fear from the Islamic State]	101
8	حتى اجدادنا يقاتلون معنا [Even our great grandfathers fight with us]	77
9	التحالف الصليبي الصفوي السلولي جاء [The Crusading, Safawi, and Salwli (Muslim hypocrites) coalition has arrived]	73
10	أول نشرة إخبارية باللغة الأوردية [First (ISIS) newscast in Urdu language]	63

11	بغل الروم يصلي إلى مريم [The Rome's mule (Obama) prays for the Virgin Mary]	53
12	أشبال الخلافة [The Caliphate's cubs (ISIS children)]	43
13	صليل الصوارم [Salil Al-Sawarim (The Clinging of the Swords chant)]	42

Note: [a]All the texts between parentheses are my translations, and the texts between brackets are further explanations.

whose Twitter accounts need to be followed or posts that they would like to have to be retweeted, such as those of @Mo7_AbuAzzam1, @isis-cyberarmy, and @Isis_Cyberarmy. In summary, ISIS tweets were mostly focused on disseminating news on its military achievements, uttering threats against its enemies as well as attacking Shiites, and Twitter remained a notably active platform for ISIS members until they were largely blocked.

Further, we wanted to understand the alleged feud between Al-Qaida and ISIS, so we used four Arabic searches related to Al-Qaeda leaders. The results revealed that 692 tweets were posted by 516 unique users in relation to Al-Qaida leaders, and Table 2.3 shows the most active and relevant Twitter accounts that referred to them, all of whom have had their Twitter accounts blocked as of February 2017. The keywords include the following: Laden (لادن) (*n*=301 tweets), Al-Zawahiri (الظواهري) (*n*=189 tweets), Al-Awlaki (العولقي) (*n*=4 tweets), and Al-Zarqawi (الزرقاوي) (*n*=198 tweets).

The findings indicate that there is a very intense feud between Al-Qaeda and ISIS on Twitter, and within this data set ISIS followers routinely call Al-Qaeda leaders and sympathizers 'Jihadi Jews' (الجهاد_يهود) in order to imply that their cause is either not truly Islamic or to associate Al-Qaeda with Israel. In fact, the

Table 2.3 The top most active Twitter users mentioning Al-Qaeda leaders

No.	*User*	*Tweet frequency*
1	m5tsrj	41
2	officeblo	12
3	isisallwrld_3	8
4	Raqqa_Sl	8
5	W2RISIS	8
6	isisallwrld_4	6
7	adghbjurvj6665	5
8	Jbhatalnusra_18	5
9	00jihad7777	4
10	isisallwrld_1	4
11	isisallwrld_2	4
12	isisallwrld_5	4
13	abobakerisis6	3

above hashtag was retweeted 37 times, often being accompanied with other hashtags like #Al-Zawahiri, #Al-Maqdissi (the Jordanian salafi leader who once mentored Al-Zarqawi), and #Abu Qumama, which is a pejorative reference to Abu Qutada al- Filistini, the famous Palestinian preacher and Al-Qaeda sympathizer.

Many other tweets carry personal attacks against Al-Zawahiri, while Al-Qaida leaders, and especially Osama Bin Laden, seem to be much more respected by ISIS followers. As examples, Al-Zarqawi and Bin Laden are often mentioned with reverence such as stating, 'Let Allah have mercy on them', and their statements are either cited or various hyperlinks to their audiovisual speeches are referenced in the tweets. Bin Laden, in particular, is given more attention as he is often called 'The Lion of the Umma' [nation] or 'The Sheikh of Mujahideen', 'the reforming Imam', and that there is 'No Al-Qaida after Bin Laden'. One tweet refers to an

ISIS operation as a revenge for Osama Bin Laden's death, while another one mentions a newly formed ISIS-run school for children that was renamed as 'Osama Bin Laden'.

On the other hand, Al-Zawahiri is repeatedly called the 'deviant' (المنحرف) and his group is labelled as 'the destroyed structure' (البنيان المهدوم). One ISIS follower, @JehadSaryah, for example, tweeted the following about Al-Qaida group: 'The Al-Zawahiri's hyenas have sharpened their knives to stab the body of the Caliphate after their scandal has been disclosed in Dabiq magazine. Let Allah paralyze them' (December 29, 2014). It is important to note here that Al-Qaida users that could be expected to defend Al- Zwahiri are almost nonexistent in the data set examined.

It is important to mention here that although the majority of those users are sympathetic toward ISIS, there are a number of other users who have trolled the terrorist group by using the same hashtags that ISIS members use. For example, Twitter user @cusois tweeted 127 times using ISIS-linked hashtags, yet the Japanese language tweets are meant to troll ISIS and make fun of its members especially with the use of memes and photoshopped images. The same applies to other users like @kuri_kerkuk (n= 103 tweets) and @abo_kafr_kurdi (n=81 tweets) who seem to be affiliated with Kurdish fighters combating ISIS and often use ISIS-related hashtags to disseminate news on the victories of Kurdish forces against the terrorist group. We believe that the rationale behind this counternarrative strategy is to demoralize ISIS members by waging a psychological warfare and showing them the grave causalities and losses the group is suffering from.

To offer more recent input about the use of Twitter by extremists, I searched for the term '#Death to America' in Arabic (#الموت_لأمريكا) using Twitter Academic API v.2 which offers a full historical archive. I found 82,891 tweets posted between September 4, 2012 and March 29, 2023. I used this term because it is mostly employed by Sunni and Shiite extremists and fierce opponents of the US- led Coalition forces in the region, and I wanted to see whether there are Twitter reactions to the killings of ISIS' three Caliphs (Abu Bakr al-Baghdadi, killed on October 27, 2019; Abu Ibrahim al-Hashimi al-Qurashi, killed on February 3, 2022; and Abu al- Hasan al- Hashimi al- Qurashi, killed on October 15, 2022). Previous studies indicate that this term is popular due to the US military interventions in the region (Rogan, 2011) and is sometimes used in chants (Patel, 2017), street graffiti, and angry protests (Browning, 2021; Hughes, 2019). In this respect, the use of 'communication- grounded research of the communiqués and writings of terrorist organizations' offers a 'useful methodological approach for discerning how terror groups construct their narratives' (Rogan, 2019, pp. 5080– 5081). Further, other relevant Arabic hashtags that were used by ISIS like (expanding) تتمدد# or (remaining) #باقية remain broad and are considered common terms used in irrelevant contexts, and their ISIS-related materials seem to be removed due to Twitter moderation policies.

Figure 2.3 shows that the highest number of tweets occurred in 2020 (n = 34,369), closely following the US killing of the Iranian General, Qassem Soleimani on January 3, 2020. Specifically, January 12, 2020 witnessed the highest number of tweets (n = 12,832) which were part of a major Twitter campaign run by Iraqi Shiite militias and their supporters who attacked Iraqi anti-government protesters for publicly celebrating the death of Soleimani. The second highest number of tweets was on January 3, 2020 (n = 2,767), the day Soleimani was killed. Despite searching for specific ISIS-related terms, the only major anti-US narratives are discussed by Shiite parties and sympathizers. In other words, ISIS seems to be largely absent from Twitter in relation to these

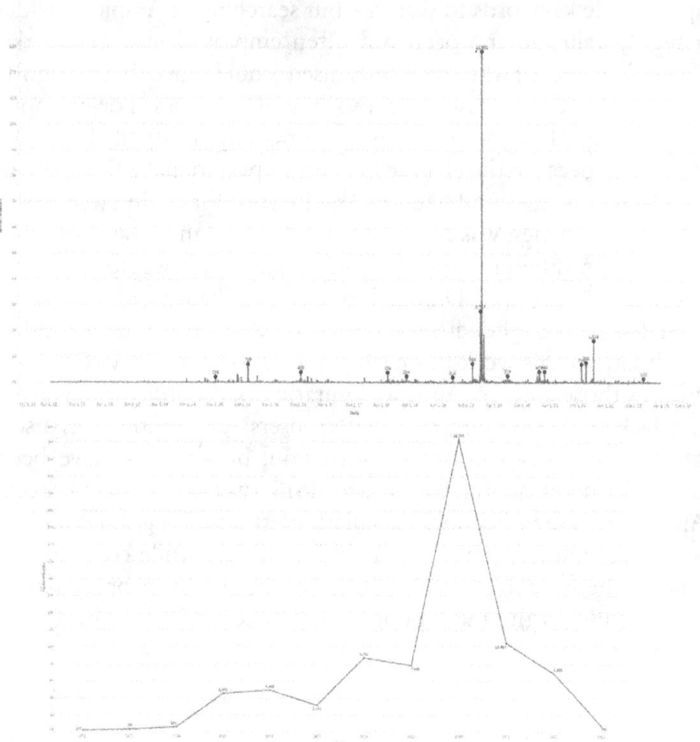

Figure 2.3 Daily tweets' distribution (top) and annual distribution (bottom).

Source: Author's creation.

anti-American discourses, mostly due to migrating to other sites, especially the Dark Web and Telegram.

In conclusion, the findings of this chapter indicate that there have been some successes and improvements in minimizing ISIS' online outreach around the time the data was collected. Still, as there are over 50 million units over a 3-year period, it remains literally impossible to completely eradicate the group's online presence on Twitter and other social media sites. As with all studies, it is also important to point out some of the limitations of this particular piece of research. Though the collected data set is very large, it has been challenging to find and research all possible appropriate keywords to search – but searching in Arabic provides a highly valuable approach not often employed in other works. Second, some of the keywords used could have been slightly changed by Twitter users for a variety of purposes. For example, the name 'Al- Zawahiri' was intentionally misspelled as 'Al-Zawaritti' because the change becomes a pun to make the name of Al-Qaeda leader sound like the Arabic word for farting (الظوارطي). This name change was difficult to detect though it was retweeted ten times by different users who disseminated a news story on how the real successor of Osama Bin Laden's jihadist campaign was Abu Bakr Al- Baghdadi rather than Al- Zawahiri. Future studies can build on this work to develop a focus on other keywords and areas as those emerge. Another limitation of the study is related to the lack of knowledge on Twitter users' geolocations as users often do not disclose such information, but it could have been useful in determining where pro- ISIS tweets originated from. Also, other emerging social media outlets like Telegram could be used to potentially trace the activities of ISIS, while comparisons among these interactive platforms can be useful in order to see which outlet is the most popular and effective in recruiting new terrorists.

Note

1 Due to a technical error, data were not collected for the period between October 11 and November 28, 2016.

References

Al-Rawi, A. (2016). Video games, terrorism, and ISIS's Jihad 3.0. *Terrorism and Political Violence*, *30*(4), 740–60.

Andrews, N., & Seetharaman, D. (2016, February 11). Facebook steps up efforts against terrorism. *The Wall Street Journal*. Retrieved from www.wsj.com/articles/facebook-steps-up-efforts-against-terrorism-1455237595

BBC News. (2015, June 22). Islamic State web accounts to be blocked by new police team. Retrieved from www.bbc.com/news/world-europe-33220037

Berger, J., & Morgan, J. (2015, March). The ISIS Twitter census: Defining and describing the population of ISIS supporters on Twitter. The Brookings Project on U.S. Relations with the Islamic World. Analysis

Paper, No. 20. Retrieved from www.brookings.edu/~/media/research/files/papers/2015/03/isis-twitter-census-berger-morgan/isis_twitter_census_berger_morgan.pdf

Borra, E., and Rieder, B. (2014). Programmed method: developing a toolset for capturing and analyzing tweets. *Aslib Journal of Information Management*, *66*(3), 262–78.

Browning, Oliver. (2021, August 16). CNN reporter describes Taliban chanting 'death to America' on streets as 'friendly'. *The Independent*. Retrieved from www.independent.co.uk/tv/news/cnn-reporter-describes-taliban-chanting-death-to-america-on-kabul-streets-as-friendly-b2181035.html

Callimachi, Rukmini. (2017, February 4). Not 'Lone Wolves' after all: How ISIS guides world's terror plots from Afar. Retrieved from www.nytimes.com/2017/02/04/world/asia/isis-messaging-app-terror-plot.html?_r=0

Castillo, W. (2015, June 5). Air Force intel uses ISIS 'moron' post to track fighters. Retrieved from www.cnn.com/2015/06/05/politics/air-force-isis-moron-twitter/

Cottee, Simon. (2015, March 2).Why it's so hard to stop ISIS propaganda. *The Atlantic*. Retrieved from www.theatlantic.com/international/archive/2015/03/why-its-so-hard-to-stop-isis-propaganda/386216/

Groshek, J. (2014). Twitter Collection and Analysis Toolkit (TCAT) at Boston University. Retrieved from www.bu.edu/com/bu-tcat/

Habeck, M. (2014). *Assessing the ISIS–al-Qaeda Split: Introduction*. New York: Soufan Group. Retrieved from http://news.siteintelgroup.com/blog/index.php/about-us/21-jihad/4388-assessing-the-isis-al-qaeda-split-introduction

Hughes, G. (2019). Tribes without Sheikhs? Technological change, media liberalization, and authority in networked Jordan. Technological Change, Media Liberalization, and Authority in Networked Jordan. Retrieved from https://ore.exeter.ac.uk/repository/bitstream/handle/10871/37553/WP24%20%28Flag%20Cover%29.pdf?sequence=1

Jeong, Sarah. (2016, February 5). Twitter: We've blocked 125,000 ISIS accounts since mid-2015. Motherboard. Retrieved from http://motherboard.vice.com/read/twitter-we-blocked-125000-isis-accounts-since-mid-2015

Klausen, J. (2015). Tweeting the Jihad: Social media networks of western foreign fighters in Syria and Iraq. *Studies in Conflict & Terrorism*, *38*(1), 1–22.

Lopatin, E., Samuel-Azran, T., & Galily, Y. (2017). A clash-of-civilizations prism in German media? Documenting a shift from political to religious framing of the Israeli–Palestinian conflict. *Communication and the Public, 2*(1), 19–34.

Mahood, S., & Rane, H. (2017). Islamist narratives in ISIS recruitment propaganda. *The Journal of International Communication, 23*(1), 15–35.

McCants, W. (September 25, 2016). The Feud between Al-Qaeda and the Islamic State, explained. *Newsweek*. Retrieved from www.newsweek.com/isis-al-qaeda-feud-499052

McConnell, D. & Todd, B. (September 11, 2015). Leader of al Qaeda belittles leader of ISIS as not worthy. *CNN*. Retrieved from https://edition.cnn.com/2015/09/11/middleeast/al-qaeda-isis-bickering/index.html

Melchior, J. (2014). ISIS tactics illustrate social media's new place in modern war. *TechCrunch*. Retrieved from: http://techcrunch.com/2014/10/15/isis-tactics-illustrate-social- medias-new-place-in-modern-war

Milton, Daniel. (2016, October 10). Communication breakdown: Unraveling the Islamic State's media efforts. Combating Terrorism Center at West Point. Retrieved from www.ctc.usma.edu/v2/wp-content/uploads/2016/10/ISMedia_Online.pdf

Patel, B. (2017). Understanding female martyrdom. *American Intelligence Journal, 34*(1), 83–96.

Rogan, R. G. (2011). "Death to America": A frame analysis of Usama bin Laden's declarations of war against the United States. In W. A Donohue, R. G. Rogan, & S. Kaufmann (Eds.), *Framing matters: Perspectives on negotiation research and practice in communication* (pp. 210–33). New York, NY: Peter Lang.

Rogan, R. G. (2019). Quest for immortality: An Analysis of ISIS's Dabiq. *International Journal of Communication, 13*, 20.

3 Video Games*

Introduction

In relation to video games and their connection to terrorism, a number of games directly deal with terror-related issues, especially in connection with the War on Terror. For example, *Splinter Cell* is a game that revolves around the 9/11 events, (Young, 2015), while *Counter-Strike* allows teams from opposing sides to take the role of terrorists as well as counterterrorists (Newman, 2008, p. 169; Wild, 2014; Wright, Boria, & Breidenbach, 2002). Similar to *Counter-Strike*, other games like *America's Army, Modern Warfare 2*, and *Medal of Honor: Warfighter* allow players to become terrorists, which could have some psychological and educational benefits (Schulzke, 2013). In 2006, Al-Qaeda group made changes to the first person shooter game *Quest for Saddam* (2003) and introduced another game called *Quest for Bush*. The goal of the original game was to kill Iraqi soldiers and capture Saddam Hussein, whereas Al-Qaeda completely reversed the players' roles. Further, the Iraqi American artist, Wafaa Bilal, made more adaptations to the same game, which he called *Night of Bush Capturing: A Virtual Jihadi* (Charles, 2009). As a social and artistic experience, Bilal's video game version created some controversy because the player was 'in the position of a suicide bomber whose aim is to kill the president of the United States' (Sweeny, 2010, p. 263).

* This chapter is largely based on a previous study whose details are as follows: Al-Rawi, A. (2018). Video games, terrorism, and ISIS's Jihad 3.0. *Terrorism and Political Violence, 30*(4), 740–60.

DOI: 10.4324/9781032615882-4

On the other hand, video games by the Lebanese Hezbollah and Syrian Afkar Media company were used as alternative media outlets to offer playing roles that were contrary to the mainstream Western representation of Arab Muslims (Sisler, 2009). In this way, 'video games provide violent non-state actors and organizations sympathetic to them with a means of presenting their grievances and displaying their fighting prowess in ways that advance the organizations' strategic goals' (Schulzke, 2015, p. 627). Some of these alternative games include *Quraish* and *Under Siege*, which were both produced by Afkar Media (Sisler, 2012).

Trolling, Flaming, and Social Media Effects

This chapter covers two concepts that are related to the use of harsh and violent language, namely, trolling and flaming. There is, however, a conceptual problem in defining these two terms because of the apparent overlap between them. In fact, 'trolling and flaming often merge, in that in both cases there is intent to disrupt the ongoing conversation, and both can lead to extended aggravated argument' (Herring et al., 2002, p. 372). In this regard, the relative anonymity of online users enhances the kind of flaming or trolling that can occur on different platforms (Suler, 2004; Lapidot-Lefler & Barak, 2012). In general, the two terms involve using some kind of negative face that is explained below by employing computer-mediated communication.

The literature on these two types of antisocial behavior is also connected to studies and reports on child protection practices. In general, there is often a sense of moral panic, risk, and public anxiety when it comes to children's Internet exposure and use (David et al., 2011; Clapton, Cree, & Smith, 2013). Social media use could have negative effects on the well-being of some adolescents including what is known as 'E-Crime 2.0', which includes 'offences that exploit the ways in which users of new communication technologies make themselves publicly visible and available through new social media' (Yar, 2012, pp. 207–08). Some of the harmful social media effects that are reported in previous research on adolescents and children include 'social isolation, depression and cyber-bullying' (Best, Manktelow, & Taylor, 2014). In a large-scale study that involved about 10,000 European Union children, the respondents themselves reported certain types of risks that they find on the Internet, including pornography, cyberbullying, and violent content (Livingstone et al., 2014). Other types of harmful effects include 'poor self-rating of mental health and experiences of high levels of psychological distress and suicidal ideation' (Sampasa-Kanyinga & Lewis, 2015). Indeed, exposure to violent content seems to be one of the main recurrent public concerns when it comes to social media use by adolescents and children.

In their politeness theory, Brown and Levinson (1987) discuss the different motivations behind using negative face. For example, it might be used when discussing 'dangerously emotional or divisive topics e.g. politics, race, religion'. Some of the goals behind employing it include certain kinds of 'orders and requests' made to denote to the other person a desire to do or refrain from doing something (p. 67). In their compliance gaining theory, Marwell and Schmitt (1967) discussed several techniques to persuade people including 'punishing activity,' which refers to the use of negative face or actions which usually entail uttering threats. Though the study was published long before the emergence of the Internet, trolling and flaming can be linked to this theoretical concept since they can be regarded as an online attempt to gain compliance by either modifying or preventing certain kinds of behavior with the persistent use of negative face.

In relation to trolling, one of the first studies that examined it was conducted by Donath (1999) on Usenet groups. Also, Hardaker (2010) provides several definitions for trolling and classifies it into different types based on four main features: aggression, deception, disruption, and success. In relation to this chapter, two categories are more relevant. The first one is called thwarted/frustrated impoliteness, which refers to the malicious intent of a message, but its intention is frustrated or thwarted by the receiver either because he/she is not offended, so no action is taken (frustrated), or because it is countered by, for example, 'sarcasm, contempt, amusement, or suchlike' (thwarted). The second type is called genuine, malicious, or strategic impoliteness, which successfully achieves its goal in offending the receiver(s). Further, Bishop (2014) discusses two types of trolling: flame trolling and kudus trolling. The former refers to vitriolic comments that are not intended to be humorous, unlike the latter type. Again, the overlap between these two terms is obvious here. Bishop also classified people who troll others into different types, yet none of the classifications he offered could be applicable to the focus of this chapter on mediated terrorism.

In all cases, trolling seeks to create an argument, entice others into endless discussion, or hijack a discussion (Baker 2001; Herring et al., 2002; Turner et al., 2005). In other words, trolling is meant as a distraction from the main online discussion in the forum or platform by diverting attention to another issue which is mostly irrelevant.

Similar to trolling, there is no agreement on a unified definition of flaming, but it usually 'consists of aggressive or hostile communication occurring via computer-mediated channels' (O'Sullivan & Flanagin, 2003). Indeed, flaming is similar to trolling, but the language is usually harsher, more personal, and is far more aggressive since it contains insults, obscenity, swearing, and curses (Moor, Heuvelman, & Verleur, 2010), especially if the topic relates to religion (Al-Rawi, 2015a, 2016a, 2016b).

Whether trolling or flaming, ISIS sympathizers run what is called '"disseminator" accounts' on social media, especially Twitter, which 'lend moral and political support to those in the conflict' (Carter, Maher, & Neumann, 2014). It is also known as the Swarmcast model in communication studies; 'once content is produced and released, it is often the distributing network of media mujahideen, rather than the original producer, that ensures continuing content availability' (Fisher, 2015). This model suggests that sympathizers gather like a swarm of bees or birds that always re-organize themselves and are ready to engage and attack at any given time. In the following section, a discussion is made on ISIS' media techniques.

ISIS' Video Game

The focus of this study is on the video game released by ISIS that is adapted from the well-known *Grand Theft Auto* (GTA). In particular, the research is limited to the videos and comments posted on this video game trailer. It is not clear whether the game was truly produced or not; it is also not clear who exactly developed it since there are many links to the video game, especially those leading to torrent websites. However, the current links either do not work or lead to malicious websites. Certainly, the video game's trailer is not produced by the centralized media centers of ISIS like Al-Hayat, Al-Furqan, and Al-Ethar, especially in that the group stands against entertainment activities like listening to music or playing games that can divert attention from prayer and faith (Ramadan, 2015). This means that the game is made by some ISIS followers or sympathizers probably outside the group's controlled territories. In terms of its development, it is not difficult to make changes to the original GTA game by customizing characters or playing opposing roles similar to *America's Army* and *Modern Warfare 2*, as mentioned above. As for the date of ISIS' video game release, one of the first videos to report on the GTA game appeared on YouTube in June 2014, but the game became more popular in September of the same year, based on a Google search in Arabic using the term 'Download Salil al-Sawarem's game'. 'Salil al-Sawarem' is also the name given by ISIS to its motivational religious chant, which must be distinguished from the video game (Al-Rawi, 2016c). In all cases, the game is called 'Salil al-Sawarem' in Arabic (The Clanging of the Swords), which is a first person shooter game (Crompton, 2014). The game's cover reads: 'Your games which are producing from you, we do the same actions in the battlefields!!' (Hall, 2014). In other words, the types of real armed confrontations ISIS is engaged with are similar to the virtual wars produced in Western video games. Further, the name itself given to the game is also supposed to project the idea of strength, fearlessness, and resilience at times of war.

It is alleged that ISIS adapted another first person shooter game called *RMA III* which is developed for Microsoft as well as another version of the famous *Call of Duty* (Kang, 2014).

In general, the target group of such video games is young people who are supposed to be more attracted to violent and first shooter games. There seems to be certain emotional appeals for young male adolescents to play first shooter games (Jansz, 2005; Jansz & Tanis, 2007), including a desire to 'experience fantasies of power and fame, to explore and master what they perceive as exciting and realistic environments (but distinct from real life), to work through angry feelings or relieve stress, and as social tools' (Olson, Kutner, & Warner, 2008). Other studies showed that there is a positive correlation between adolescents' anger, frustration, and peer rejection on the one hand and preference for antisocial media content and cyberbullying on the other hand (Plaisier &

Konijn, 2013; Den Hamer, Konijn, & Keijer, 2014). Indeed, violent video games are more appealing for adolescents than for adults (Griffiths, Davies, & Chappell, 2004), partly due to the wishful identification with some of the games' characters (Konjin, Bijvank, & Bushman, 2007). As mentioned above, some view ISIS as a 'cool' organization in its Jihad 3.0 efforts, so producing such games can help in recruiting young people to its organization.

In terms of methodology, an Arabic-language search was made on YouTube using the term 'ISIS's Salil al-Sawarem game' on September 5, 2015. YouTube is selected because it is regarded as one of the most famous video platforms in the world (Burgess & Green, 2013), and YouTube gaming channels that attract people from different ages, especially teenagers, are regarded as the most popular ones (Miller, 2012). In fact, YouTube gaming offers massive economic opportunities for video game producers and professional gamers because of the large number of fans (Zoia, 2014).

The top ten clips were selected based on the number of views (see Table 3.1) (Al-Rawi, 2016d, 2016e), and a content analysis of the posted videos and their comments was conducted to understand their tone or valence in terms of expressing negative, positive, or neutral views toward the game and its sponsor (Krippendorff, 2012; Riffe, Lacy, & Fico, 2014). The tone of the video toward ISIS and its video game was assessed based on what is presented in the video itself, the title, and/or its accompanying description. This is a method that has been followed in many studies on YouTube videos and their comments (Mosemghvdlishvili & Jansz, 2012; Thelwall, Sud, & Vis, 2012; Van Zoonen, Vis, & Mihelj, 2010; Al-Rawi, 2014).

In relation to this chapter, video clips (8) and (9) mostly presented the game in a neutral way, yet their descriptions referred to ISIS as a state that must remain forever (*Baqyyah* #باقية), or that it was the one which follows the right path of Prophet Muhammed. Hence, these two videos were coded as positive toward ISIS and the game. If the stance was not clear, the video was coded as neutral. Before coding all the videos and comments, two coders examined over 10% of the sample (n = 3 videos and 50 comments), and intercoder reliability was measured using Cohen's Kappa. A .890 agreement was reached that was very acceptable (Landis & Koch, 1977).

Table 3.1 YouTube clips on ISIS' video game

No.	*No. of views*	*Tone*	*No. of comments*	*Date posted*	*No. of likes*	*No. of dislikes*
1	119,814	Negative	196	Oct 8, 2014	1,154	254
2	37,552	Positive	6	Sep 21, 2014	176	291
3	37,256	Positive	14	Sep 21, 2014	73	29
4	27,853	Positive	83	Jul 8, 2015	117	143
5	12,952	Positive	Disabled	Sep 21, 2014	31	78
6	11,844	Neutral	13	Sep 20, 2014	34	31
7	11,096	Neutral	17	Mar 13, 2015	25	94
8	10,654	Positive	5	Aug 7, 2015	58	29
9	9,576	Positive	20	Jun 7, 2014	78	39
10	8,091	Negative	43	Oct 17, 2014	56	55

The total number of views for these ten videos was 286,688 and the earliest clip posted was on June 7, 2014. The highest number of views (119,861) and comments (196) was for a video that made fun of the game and ISIS that was posted by an Iraqi comedian who imitates Jon Stewart and Bassem Youssef. As for the tone of posted videos, there were more positive clips toward ISIS and its video game (n = 6) than negative (n = 2) or neutral (n = 2) ones. In fact, some video posters openly showed their support for ISIS. For example, video clip number (2) is posted by user 'Abu Bakr Al-Baghdadi's lovers,' while many other commentators have ISIS' black banner as their users' photo. With regard to the total number of likes and dislikes, it was only accurate to count them by taking into account the tone of the videos posted. In total, there were 1,944 dislikes (68.3%) of the game and ISIS in comparison to 901 likes (31.5%).

As for the comments, there were a total of 397 comments and replies on the posted videos. Due to the highly personal nature of replies, they were discarded from the study together with any irrelevant and ambiguous posts. In total, 199 comments were identified; 57.2% (n = 114) of the comments were negative toward the game and ISIS, 33.6% (n = 67) comments were positive, and 9% (n = 18) were neutral without supporting any side. With regard to the negative comments, they usually contained praise for anyone who criticized ISIS and its game, which was usually ridiculed for the claim that it was independently developed from *Grand Theft Auto*. For example, YouTuber 'Hadji M' mentioned that 'this is a famous American video game, and any person with some experience in programming can change the shapes of its characters and even the sound effects.' Further, most of the criticism was centered on showing that ISIS did not represent Islam and/or that Shiite militias fighting ISIS were victorious. As for the positive comments that praised the game and ISIS, they constituted 33.6% of the total comments. These results closely correspond with the number of video dislikes (68.3%) of the game and their likes (31.5%). Despite the dominance of negative comments against ISIS, there was still an active group of sympathizers and followers who mostly believed that supporting ISIS online was an expression of their devotion to Sunni Islam, allegedly under attack by Shiites. To give a few examples, YouTuber 'Islamic Flood' says:

> You've reached a cowardice stage that you're afraid of an Islamic State's game. Hail to the Islamic state's men and let [Allah] fortify its Mujahideen. The Islamic State has defeated you in all the religious, military, cultural and even electronic fronts.

Another YouTuber called 'Muhammed Al-Mutairi' gave ISIS a more regional scope, stating: 'We wish the game's objective is to make the Mujahideen heroes'.

Their goal is to spread Islam, defend the righteous, and lift injustice from Muslims. Frankly, we need such games in order to have a new generation whose goal is to remove Israel and its agents from Muslim lands. Finally, YouTuber 'Hasoon A' connected his favorable comment toward ISIS with famous Twitter hashtags such as 'ISIS remains' that is mentioned above, saying: 'It'll expand (#تمتد); if you leave it alone, it'll be strengthened (#تشتد). By Allah's will, if you fight it, it'll remain (#باقية).'

As mentioned above, almost all the replies were personal, containing attacks on individual posters who opposed ISIS or vice versa. These replies were highly sectarian in nature as there was intense flaming in the kind of exchange of obscene language and religious curses especially between Sunnis and Shiites. For example, any criticism against ISIS was interpreted by some of the group's sympathizers as criticism against Islam and/or the Sunni faith. This finding is similar to other studies that examined religious comments on YouTube and the divisive sectarian rhetoric that characterizes this platform (Al-Rawi, 2015). The prevalent use of the negative face by the two opposing online communities was expected because of the nature of the religious topic discussed (Brown & Levinson, 1987). The main function of the negative face was to gain compliance via punishing activity (Marwell & Schmitt, 1967). This was routinely done by using flaming in order to either force the opponents to leave the platform/video commentary section or make them stop writing negative comments.

Further and in relation to the swarming communication model, ISIS followers seemed to gather around videos that referred to Daesh (داعش), which is the Arabic acronym of ISIS. The term itself is regarded as demeaning by ISIS, which prohibits people living under its control from using it (Garrity, 2015). ISIS followers are usually very active in responding to ISIS criticism and are often accompanied by other users who share the same beliefs. Similar to a swarming activity, they closely coordinate and synchronize their trolls as they suddenly appear to assist some ISIS members in the exchange of insults, and they disappear afterward. It is like waging a constant online war.

The other main function of this trolling activity is to silence opposition and dissent, especially that which comes from Shiite Muslims. Most importantly, the trolling and flaming game played by ISIS followers on YouTube serves the purpose of winning some oppositional or neutral voices to their side since the exchange of insults frequently results in curses against Sunni figures who are highly venerated, like Prophet Mohammed's companions. In this way, ISIS followers will get the required evidence that Shiites hold antagonistic views against Sunnis, which might produce the possible impact on some devout Sunnis. This sophisticated technique is similar to what is used by ISIS on English language platforms that target Westerners such as the case of Twitter. Further, other news reports that are widely shared on social media like 'US Gunmaker Creates "Crusader" Rifle to Fight Islamic State' (Web Desk, 2015) are regarded by ISIS as excellent examples that support their abovementioned claim.

In this regard, this trolling and flaming game, which I call the 'troll, flame, and engage' technique, is regarded as an effective recruitment tool in ISIS' Jihad 3.0 efforts. It is important to note here that some of the attempts made by ISIS followers and sympathizers to create a reaction from the online audience fail in what is called thwarted/frustrated impoliteness (Hardaker, 2010). These attempts to agitate YouTubers are meant to be tactical diversions from the main negative discussion on and criticism of ISIS, which is what characterizes trolling (Baker, 2001). Yet, a few other attempts by ISIS followers can be categorized as genuine, malicious, or strategic impoliteness (Hardaker, 2010) because they succeed in offending their opponents by using highly obscene terms, insults, and curses. For example, one YouTuber, 'Layth Jamal,' systematically flames by posting abusive comments in response to anyone criticizing ISIS in order to gain compliance. He starts trolling one user, 'Abdulla ahmmad12', and is suddenly accompanied by YouTuber 'Gvhh Gbj', who both personally attack and succeed in offending their target. In the end, they engage him by using sectarian rhetoric which is meant to gain his support, silence him, or force him to abandon the online platform. In the example given here, 'Abdulla ahmmad12' starts questioning 'Layth Jamal' for the latter's flaming language.

In his response, 'Layth Jamal' says: 'I have started insulting any Shiite I encounter online though they still post negative comments against me' because he praises ISIS. In this case, 'Layth Jamal' believes that flaming can drive users away from the platform or from posting negative comments. Further, the sectarian language was meant to engage others, for 'Abdulla ahmmad12' responded by saying: 'By Allah, I'm a Sunni myself'. 'Layth Jamal' further manipulated the sectarian discussion by questioning 'Abdulla ahmmad12''s faith: 'If you are a Sunni, how come you encourage them to make such offensive clips that insult the Prophet. The Shiites sent me private messages in which they cursed Abu Bakr, Othman, and Aysha [Muhammed's companions]'. Further, 'Gvhh Gbj' offered his apology for flaming, stating that he thought that 'Abdulla ahmmad12' was a 'dirty and filthy Shiite.' The online engagement ended with a cheerful tone due to reaching some kind of mutual understanding. In brief, 'Layth Jamal' and 'Gvhh Gbj' made use of the anonymous feature of YouTube to swarm and troll others whenever they found a suitable video that demeaned ISIS. The purpose was to divert attention from the main discussion, and flaming was used if the impoliteness was thwarted or frustrated, which ultimately ended in engaging some neutral or opposing voices.

In conclusion, the general goal behind making and releasing Salil al-Sawarem's video game was to gain publicity and attract attention to the group. This is part of the group's Jihad 3.0 efforts, as the main target is young people who might get the impression that ISIS is a technologically advanced group that not only produces high-definition and well-edited videos but also has its own apps, social media tools, drones, and video games. The findings of this chapter show that, at the time of conducting this study, the majority of comments and number of likes and dislikes were against ISIS and its video game, but YouTube remained one of the main online platforms wherein ISIS was still sharing and spreading its messages, which is clearly evident in the high number of favorable ISIS videos. Also, there were a considerable number of followers and sympathizers who constantly tried to influence others by using trolls, flames, and certain kinds of engagements, while a highly divisive and sectarian rhetoric was used in order to polarize the audience and possibly gain the support of some neutral users.

For future research, more studies are needed to examine other online platforms in order to investigate whether swarming and the troll, flame, and engage method are also used by ISIS followers. Furthermore, interviews with online users who are actively engaged with ISIS members are needed to extend the understanding of various motivations and possible effects of this online interaction with a focus on gender, sectarian discussion, and age.

References

Al-Rawi, A. (2014). Cyber warriors in the Middle East: The case of the Syrian electronic army. *Public Relations Review*, *40*(3), 420–28. https://doi.org/10.1016/j.pubrev.2014.04.005

Al-Rawi, A. (2015). Sectarianism and the Arab Spring: Framing the popular protests in Bahrain. *Global Media and Communication*, *11*(1), 25–42. https://doi.org/10.1177/1742766515573550

Al-Rawi, A. (2016a). Facebook as a virtual mosque: The online protest against innocence of Muslims. *Culture and Religion*, *17*(1), 19–34. https://doi.org/10.1080/14755610.2016.1159591

Al-Rawi, A. (2016b). The online response to the Quran burning incidents. In N. Mellor & K. Rinnawi (Eds.), *Political Islam and global media: The boundaries of religious identity* (pp. 105–21). Routledge. http://dx.doi.org/10.4324/9781315637129-7

Al-Rawi, A. (2016c). Anti-ISIS humor: Cultural resistance of radical ideology. *Politics, Religion & Ideology*, *17*(1), 52–68. https://doi.org/10.1080/21567689.2016.1157076

Al-Rawi, A. (2016d). Assessing public sentiments and news preferences on Al Jazeera and Al Arabiya. *International Communication Gazette*, *79*(1), 1–19. http://dx.doi.org/10.1177/1748048516642732

Al-Rawi, A. (2016e). Understanding the social media audiences of radio stations. *Journal of Radio & Audio Media*, *23*(1), 50–67. https://doi.org/10.1080/19376529.2016.1155298

Baker, P. (2001). Moral panic and alternative identity construction in Usenet. *Journal of Computer-Mediated Communication*, *7*(1). https://doi.org/10.1111/j.1083-6101.2001.tb00136.x

Best, P., Manktelow, R., & Taylor, B. (2014). Online communication, social media and adolescent wellbeing: A systematic narrative review. *Children and Youth Services Review*, *41*, 27–36. https://doi.org/10.1016/j.childyouth.2014.03.001

Bishop, J. (2014). Representations of 'trolls' in mass media communication: A review of media-texts and moral panics relating to 'Internet trolling.' *International Journal of Web Based Communities*, *10*(1), 12. http://dx.doi.org/10.1504/IJWBC.2014.058384

Brown, P., & Levinson, S. C. (1987). *Politeness: Some universals in language usage*. Cambridge University Press.

Burgess J., & Green, J. (2013). *YouTube: Online video and participatory culture*. Wiley & Sons.

Carter, J. A., Maher, S., & Neumann, P. R. (2014). *#Greenbirds: Measuring importance and influence in Syrian Foreign Fighter Networks*. The International Centre for the Study of Radicalisation and Political Violence. http://icsr.info/wp-content/uploads/2014/04/ICSR-Report-Greenbirds-Measuring-Importance-and-Infleunce-in-Syrian-Foreign-Fighter-Networks.pdf

Charles, A. (2009). Playing with one's self: Notions of subjectivity and agency in digital games. *Eludamos. Journal for Computer Game Culture*, *3*(2), 281–94. https://septentrio.uit.no/index.php/eludamos/index

Clapton, G., Cree, V. E., & Smith, M. (2013). Moral panics and social work: Towards a sceptical view of UK child protection. *Critical Social Policy*, *33*(2), 197–217. https://doi.org/10.1177/0261018312457860

Crompton, P. (2014, September 20). Grand Theft Auto: ISIS? Militants reveal video game. *Al Arabiya*. http://english.alarabiya.net/en/variety/2014/09/20/Grand-Theft-Auto-ISIS-Militants-reveal-video-game.html

David, M., Rohloff, A., Petley, J., & Hughes, J. (2011. The idea of moral panic—Ten dimensions of dispute. *Crime, Media, Culture*, *7*(3), 215–28. https://doi.org/10.1177/1741659011417601

Den Hamer, A., Konijn, E. A., & Keijer, M. G. (2014). Cyberbullying behavior and adolescents' use of media with antisocial content: A cyclic process model. *Cyberpsychology, Behavior, and Social Networking*, *17*(2), 74–81. https://doi.org/10.1089/cyber.2012.0307

Donath, J. S. (1999). Identity and deception in the virtual community. In P. Kollock & M. Smith (Eds.), *Communities in cyberspace* (pp. 27–58). London: Routledge.

Fisher, A. (2015). Swarmcast: How Jihadist networks maintain a persistent online presence. *Perspectives on Terrorism*, *9*(3), 4. www.jstor.org/stable/26297378

Garrity, P. (2015, November 14). Paris attacks: What does 'Daesh' mean and why does ISIS hate it? *NBC News*. www.nbcnews.com/storyline/isis-terror/paris-attacks-what-does-daesh-mean-why-does-isis-hate-n463551

Griffiths, M. D., Davies, M. N. O., & Chappell, D. (2004). Online computer gaming: A comparison of adolescent and adult gamers. *Journal of Adolescence, 27*(1), 87–96. https://psycnet.apa.org/doi/10.1016/j.adolescence.2003.10.007

Hall, M. (2014, November 1). 'This is our call of duty': How ISIS is using video games. Salon. www.salon.com/2014/11/01/this_is_our_call_of_duty_how_isis_is_using_video_games/

Hardaker, C. (2010). Trolling in asynchronous computer-mediated communication: From user discussions to academic definitions. *Journal of Politeness Research, 6*(2), 215–42. https://doi.org/10.1515/jplr.2010.011

Herring, S., Job-Sluder, K., Scheckler, R., & Barab, S. (2002). Searching for safety online: Managing 'trolling' in a feminist forum. *The Information Society, 18*(5), 371–84. https://doi.org/10.1080/01972240290108186

Jansz, J. (2005). The emotional appeal of violent video games for adolescent males. *Communication Theory, 15*(3), 219–41. https://psycnet.apa.org/doi/10.1111/j.1468-2885.2005.tb00334.x

Jansz, J., & Tanis, M. (2007). Appeal of playing online first person shooter games. *CyberPsychology & Behavior, 10*(1), 133–6. https://psycnet.apa.org/doi/10.1089/cpb.2006.9981

Kang, J. C. (2014, September 18). ISIS's call of duty. *The New Yorker.* www.newyorker.com/tech/elements/isis-video-game

Konjin, E. A., Bijvank, M. N., & Bushman, B. J. (2007). I wish I were a warrior: The role of wishful identification in the effects of violent video games on aggression in adolescent boys. *Developmental Psychology, 43*(4), 1038. https://doi.org/10.1037/0012-1649.43.4.1038

Krippendorff, K. (2012). *Content analysis: An introduction to its methodology.* Sage.

Landis, J. R., & Koch, G. G. (1977). The measurement of observer agreement for categorical data. *Biometrics, 33*(1), 159–74. https://doi.org/10.2307/2529310

Lapidot-Lefler, N., & Barak, A. (2012). Effects of anonymity, invisibility, and lack of eye-contact on toxic online disinhibition. *Computers in Human Behavior, 28*(2), 434–43. https://psycnet.apa.org/doi/10.1016/j.chb.2011.10.014

Livingstone, S., Kirwil, L., Ponte, C., & Staksrud, E. (2014). In their own words: What bothers children online? *European Journal of Communication, 29* (3), 271–88. https://doi.org/10.1177/0267323114521045

Marwell, G., & Schmitt, D. R. (1967). Dimensions of compliance-gaining behavior: An empirical analysis. *Sociometry, 30*(4), 350–64. https://doi.org/10.2307/2786181

Miller, K. (2012). *Playing along: Digital games, YouTube, and virtual performance.* Oxford University Press.

Moor, P. J., Heuvelman, A., & Verleur, R. (2010). Flaming on Youtube. *Computers in Human Behavior*, *26*(6), 1536–46. https://psycnet.apa.org/doi/10.1016/j.chb.2010.05.023

Mosemghvdlishvili, L., & Jansz, J. (2012). Framing and praising Allah on YouTube: Exploring user-created videos about Islam and the motivations for producing them. *New Media & Society*, *15*(4), 482–500. https://doi.org/10.1177/1461444812457326

Newman, J. (2008). *Playing with videogames*. London: Routledge.

Olson, C. K., Kutner, L. A., & Warner, D. E. (2008). The role of violent video game content in adolescent development: Boys' perspectives. *Journal of Adolescent Research*, *23*(1), 55. https://doi.org/10.1177/0743558407310713

O'Sullivan P. B., & Flanagin, A. J. (2003). Reconceptualizing 'flaming' and other problematic messages. *New Media & Society*, *5*(1), 70. https://psycnet.apa.org/doi/10.1177/1461444803005001908

Plaisier, X. S., & Konijn, E. A. (2013). Rejected by peers—Attracted to antisocial media content: Rejection-based anger impairs moral judgment among adolescents. *Developmental Psychology*, *49*(6), 1165–73. https://psycnet.apa.org/doi/10.1037/a0029399

Ramadan, A. (2015, August 21). After the Internet, TV is next on ISIS blacklist. *The Arab Weekly*. www.thearabweekly.com/?id=1634

Riffe, D., Lacy, S., & Fico, F. (2014). *Analyzing media messages: Using quantitative content analysis in research*. Routledge.

Sampasa-Kanyinga, H., & Lewis, R. F. (2015). Frequent use of social networking sites is associated with poor psychological functioning among children and adolescents. *Cyberpsychology, Behavior, and Social Networking*, *18*(7), 380–85. https://doi.org/10.1089/cyber.2015.0055

Schulzke, M. (2013). The virtual war on terror: Counterterrorism narratives in video games. *New Political Science*, *35*(4), 586–603. https://doi.org/10.1080/07393148.2013.848703

Schulzke, M. (2015). Simulating terrorism and insurgency: Video games in the war of ideas. *Cambridge Review of International Affairs*, *27*(4), 627–43. https://doi.org/10.1080/09557571.2014.960508

Sisler, V. (2009). Palestine in pixels: The Holy Land, Arab-Israeli conflict, and reality construction in video games. *Middle East Journal of Culture and Communication*, *2*(2), 275–92. http://dx.doi.org/10.1163/187398509X12476683126509

Sisler, V. (2012). Playing Muslim hero: Construction of identity in video games. In H. Campbell (Ed.), *Digital religion: Understanding religious practice in new media worlds* (pp. 136–46). Routledge.

Suler, J. (2004). The online disinhibition effect. *Cyberpsychology & Behavior*, *7* (3), 321–26. http://dx.doi.org/10.1089/1094931041291295

Sweeny, R. W. (2010). Pixellated play: Practical and theoretical issues regarding videogames in art education. *Studies in Art Education*, *51*(3), 263. http://dx.doi.org/10.1080/00393541.2010.11518807

Thelwall, M., Sud, P., & Vis, F. (2012). Commenting on YouTube videos: From Guatemalan rock to El Big Bang. *Journal of the American Society for Information Science and Technology*, *63*(3), 616–29. https://doi.org/10.1002/asi.21679

Turner, T. C., Smith, M. A., Fisher, D., & Welser, H. T. (2005). Picturing Usenet: Mapping computer-mediated collective action. *Journal of Computer-Mediated Communication*, *10*(4), Article 7. http://dx.doi.org/10.1111/j.1083-6101.2005.tb00270.x

Van Zoonen, L., Vis, F., & Mihelj, S. (2010). Performing citizenship on YouTube: activism, satire and online debate around the anti-Islam video *Fitna*. *Critical Discourse Studies*, *7*(4), 249–62. https://doi.org/10.1080/17405904.2010.511831

Web Desk. (2015, September 5). US gun-maker creates 'Crusader' rifle to fight Islamic State. *The Express Tribune*. http://tribune.com.pk/story/951268/us-gun-maker-creates-crusader-rifle-to-fight-islamic-state/

Wild, P. (2014). Sam Fisher and the 'war on terror': An analysis of *Splinter Cell* in a post-9/11 context. *Critical Studies on Terrorism*, *7*(3), 434–45. http://dx.doi.org/10.1080/17539153.2014.953309

Wright, T., Boria, E., & Breidenbach, P. (2002). Creative player actions in FPS online video games: Playing counter-strike. *Game Studies*, *2*(2), 103–23.

Yar, M. (2012). E-Crime 2.0: The criminological landscape of new social media. *Information & Communications Technology Law*, *21*(3), 207–19. https://doi.org/10.1080/13600834.2012.744224

Young, R. (2015). Going fifth freedom: Fighting the war on terror in the *Splinter Cell: Blacklist* video game. *Critical Studies on Terrorism*, *8*(1), 147–62. https://doi.org/10.1080/17539153.2015.1009750

Zoia, C. (2014, March 14). This guy makes millions playing video games on YouTube. *The Atlantic*. www.theatlantic.com/business/archive/2014/03/this-guy-makes-millions-playing-video-games-on-youtube/284402/

4 Educational Apps*

Introduction

This chapter deals with ISIS and its state-building efforts with the assistance of educational apps. Previous media studies on ISIS have not focused on the theoretical concept of state building in relation to mobile apps, for the terrorist organization aimed at building an imagined Islamic state with the assistance of media propaganda. The chapter fills a major gap in research as there are no previous empirical studies that focused on these educational apps and their jihadist objectives. I argue here that the terrorist group, ISIS, aimed at providing well-designed and executed apps that do not only offer important language and religious teaching, but also aim at *jihadizing* children into believing in militant jihad, hatred of non-Muslims, and other beliefs that ISIS held. The goal is to use such educational apps that offer standard leaning objectives and language to assist in the nation-state building efforts of ISIS.

As stated earlier, most of the state building endeavors by ISIS are standardized since they can be observed in the different cities (*willayat*) that the group controls, which means that it requires a collective effort. Besides, standardization gives legitimacy to the group's brand and projects it as fearful establishment especially if continuous violence and intimidation are practiced. The

* This chapter is largely based on a previous study whose details are as follows: Al-Rawi, A. (2023). Terrorism education in ISIS's use of children's mobile apps. In Christoph Günther (ed.). *Disentagling Jihad, Political Violence, and Media* (pp. 1–20). Edinburgh: Edinburgh University Press.

DOI: 10.4324/9781032615882-5

general goal is to subdue the masses with fear tactics, erase the previous cultural heritage and spaces, and cleanse society of unwanted members. To do so, ISIS used its own hybrid version of salafist Islam (Hassan, 2016) and standardized media productions in order to achieve its nation-building goals. In this respect, Mohammed Saad, a Syrian activist who was once imprisoned and tortured by ISIS, rightly mentioned that the group is a 'criminal gang pretending to be a state' (Liptak, 2016). This type of pretense can be linked to Anderson's 'imagined communities' concept (2006), and Berman and Shapiro are correct in observing that ISIS is 'a failed state in the making' (2015).

This chapter attempts to investigate how ISIS used its educational apps in order to assist in its state-building efforts and propaganda. In this respect, the terrorist group seems to follow standardized and systematic state-building policies which are largely borrowed from the Baath's regime strategies in Syria and Iraq. In its utopian objective in creating a Caliphate, ISIS attempted to establish another type of an imagined state, especially that one of its goals was allegedly to demolish the Sykes-Picot Agreement (1916). This new envisioned state which I call 'the Jihadist Ummah' represented ISIS' vision of a militant and extremist ideology, and the terrorist group attempts to do this by using its own standardized media and radical version of Islam as a unifier especially in imposing assimilation policies.

As mentioned in Chapter 1, ISIS' Diwan al-Ta'leem, or the Teaching Ministry, was responsible for developing new curriculum and replacing the older ones introduced by the Syrian and Iraqi governments. Then, the Committee for the Development of Curricula and Textbooks was established in September 2014 to support ISIS' efforts to create its new militant curriculum (Arvisais et al., 2021, p. 2). In general, ISIS wanted to shape children's minds and indoctrinate them with their militant, hateful, and violent ideology and propaganda (Olidort, 2016; Townsend, 2016).

In this regard, the term 'Ashbal Al Khilafa' (Caliphate's cubs) is incidentally similar to the name given to children during Saddam Hussein's rule, especially those enrolled in Uday Saddam Hussein's militia, Fedayeen Saddam. Staring in the 1990s, these military trained children were called 'Ashbal Al Qaeyd' or 'Ashbal Saddam' (President's cubs or Saddam's cubs) (Singer, 2003). As part of its standardization policy, ISIS followed between 2014 and 2017 the same educational policies throughout its controlled territories (Arvisais & Guidère, 2020, p. 498; Gadais et al., 2022, p. 3) using a systematic method of delivering exams throughout the school year with clear emphasis on teaching Islamic thought, Arabic language, English language starting from grade 4, and computer literacy starting from the first year in the intermediate level. For example, a student is expected to graduate at the age of 15 after spending 5 years in primary school starting from age 6, 2 years in the intermediate level, and 2 other years in secondary school. All school textbooks should stress militant ideology as well as strict Islamic learning and should use the Hijra calendar when referencing Islamic holidays as the standard that needs to be followed. ISIS, in other words, wanted to militarize a whole generation of children and the whole society in order to mobilize its members and prepare them to protect the terrorist group. This observation aligns with previous research on ISIS curriculum whose goal is to 'further its political and religious agenda, although in very different ways like militarization, banalization of violence and the establishment of its complex and extreme but also fragile Islamic doctrine' (Arvisais et al., 2021, p. 1).

Though not related to educational apps, Deslandes-Martineau et al.'s (2022) study examined ISIS' educational curriculum with a focus on programming textbooks. These are regarded as complementary programs offered by the terrorist group to train students on how to code and create apps using the Scratch software. Similar to the findings of this chapter, the study finds that the programming curriculum is 'rich in elements of military and religious indoctrination and effectively participates in the indoctrination of students by helping to inculcate values consistent with ISIS's jihadist ideology' (2022). In other words, the goal of the textbook seems to be more focused on enhancing extremist thought and less on developing programming and problem-solving skills.

Unlike the earlier social media activities and posts by ISIS that largely operated without clear centralization or hierarchical structure (Melchior, 2014), the centralization of ISIS' media productions is meant to standardize the message; this becomes an integral part of the state-building effort and branding a unified image. In relation to these educational mobile apps, they are considered mediascapes that function as deterritorialized third spaces (Appadurai, 1990; Bhabha, 1994), for space and physical presence are secondary, while consumption of mobile apps becomes the primary virtual bridge (Urry, 2002) connecting children and ISIS. In other words, mobile educational apps are virtual spaces where culture is transmitted in appealing ways (Al-Rawi, 2020).

In terms of method and as mentioned in Chapter 1, one of the main data sources has been ISIS' publishing agency that is known as Al-Himmah Library which has not been well researched in previous studies despite the fact that it ran several educational apps targeting children and published hundreds of books. This chapter analyzes four children's educational mobile apps used by ISIS (Letters, [formed of two parts], Night and Day Supplications, and Alphabet Teacher) that are produced by Al-Himmah Library. To run the educational apps, I used Bluestacks software on desktop computer. In terms of method, I used the Walkthrough method (Light, Burgess, & Duguay, 2018) that discusses the different features of each app, and I provide a description and contextualization of these apps supported by screenshots. This method examines among many aspects of the apps' 'embedded cultural meanings and implied ideal users and uses' (Light, Burgess, & Duguay, 2018, p. 881) as well as provides some 'interpretative aspects' that are 'underpinned by specific theoretical frameworks' (p. 882). In 2018, I also collected six school textbooks produced by ISIS from the website Archive.org in order to compare the educational apps with these textbooks that were used in the territories controlled by this terrorist group.

The findings of this chapter indicate that the majority of the messages found on the educational apps are focused on Arabic language teaching as well as Islamic jurisdiction following the group's strict interpretation of Islam. First, it is important to shed some light on the standard textbooks produced by ISIS. As Figures 4.1 and 4.2 show, there is clear emphasis on military training and militarizing children's minds by focusing on warfare training and showcasing weapons even in mundane subjects like mathematics and science.

Second, we can find a very strict application of Islamic teaching by, for example, blurring the faces of all humans and even animals because it could illicit idolatry. On the educational apps, there are no images but only animated pictures.

1- مدّ اليدين إلى الأعلى مع الوقوف على رؤوس الأصابع مع أخذ نفس عميق مَنّ الأنّف (الشهيق) و كتمّه قليلاً ثم اخراج النَّفَس مَنّ الفم ببطء مع نزول الجسم ببطء و راخاء اليدين لأسفل قريباً مَنّ القدمين مع بقاء الساقين مستقيمتين تشبه حالةّ الركوع في الصلاة .

2- مدّ اليدين إلى الأمامّ مع أنّحناء الجسم كهيئة الركوع في الصلاة مع شد الجسم إلى الأمامّ و إلى الخلف مط الجسم إلى الأمامّ وإلى اليمين و إلى اليسار .

3- فتح الذراعين جانًباً مع أخذ نفس عميق مَنّ الأنّف و كتمّه قليلاً مَنّ ثم إرخاء اليدين ببطء و اخراج النَّفّس مَنّ الفم ببطء .

4- إرخاء اليدين و القدمين بنفس الوقت بنفضهم .

7

Figure 4.1 ISIS' physical education textbook for level 2 secondary and intermediate schools.

Source: archive.org.

البندقية الخفيفة الكلاشنكوف

نبذة تاريخية على البندقية

هو سلاح فردي يرمي دراكاً و رشاً و يستعمل للاشتبكات القريبة جُرّبَ لأوّل مرّة في عام 1947 و كأنَّ اسمه العلمي (47KA) وفي عام 1950 بدأ أنّتاج هذه البندقية بكميّات كبيرة، وفي عام 1955 أدخل هذا السلاح للخدمة في الجيش الروسي كسلاح فردي رئيسي لأفراد المشاة

ويعتبر هذا السلاح مَنَ أفضل أسلحة الاقتحام الآلية مَنَّ حيثُ القوّة و التحمّل لذلك تجده يستخدم مَنَ قبل أكثر مَنَ أربعين جيشاً نظامَياً في العالم و مَنَّ اكثر الحركات الثورية و الجهادية لكفاءته ومتأنّته مع كثرة استخدامه و عمره الطويل

و هو سلاح روسي الصنع و كثير مَنَ دول العالم تقوم بصناعته مثل رومانية و بلغارية و البرتغال و كورية الشمالية و الصين و إيرانَّ و السعودية و باكستانَّ و ألمانيا و غيرها

38

Figure 4.1 (Continued)

قواعد التنشين

1- تقدير المسافة بينك و بين الهدف و ضبط المسافة على مسطرة المسفات

2- إمساك السلاح جيّداً بحيثُ تكوّن متمَكّناً منه

3- التنشين على الهدف بحيثُ تكوّن الشعيرة في منتصف الفريضة على نفس مستوى الارتفاع في منتصف الهدف

4- حاول أنَّ تكتمَ نفسك و لكن بدون تكلّف

5- اعصر الزناد عصراً خفيفاً حتى تخرج الطلقة و أنَت لا تشعر و لا تنتش

6- لاتنتظر خروج الطلقة

7- لاتمَسك السلاح بشدة (عدم التشنج)

8- يكون التنشين بالعين اليمنى لمَن يَرمي باليد اليمنى و التنشين بالعين اليسرى لمَنَّ يرمي باليد اليسرى

48

Figure 4.1 (Continued)

حيوانات آكلة الأعشاب   حيوانات آكلة اللحوم

غذاء النبات

النبات هو المصدر الأساسي في غذاء الإنسان والحيوان في البيئة.

سؤال: كيف يحصل النبات على غذائه؟

ج / النبات يصنع غذاءَه بنفسه.

أوراق النباتات هي التي تصنع الغذاء ، وتحتاج إلى الماء وغاز ثنائي أوكسيد الكاربون بمساعدة ضوء الشمس والمادة الخضراء. النبات يصنع غذاءَه لنفسه ، وللإنسان والحيوان.

وهكذا نرى أنّ العلاقة بينَ الكائنات الحيّة (إنسان وحيوان ونبات) في البيئة هي علاقة غذائيّة. الإنسان والحيوان فيها (الآكل)، والنبات فيها (المأكول).

إنّ النباتَ هو المصدر الأساسي في غذاء الإنسان والحيوانات في البيئة. نوع العلاقة بينَ الكائنات الحيّة في البيئةِ هي علاقة (آكل ومأكول) وتأخذ العلاقة شكل سلسلة

13

Figure 4.2 ISIS' science textbook for Grade 4.

Source: archive.org.

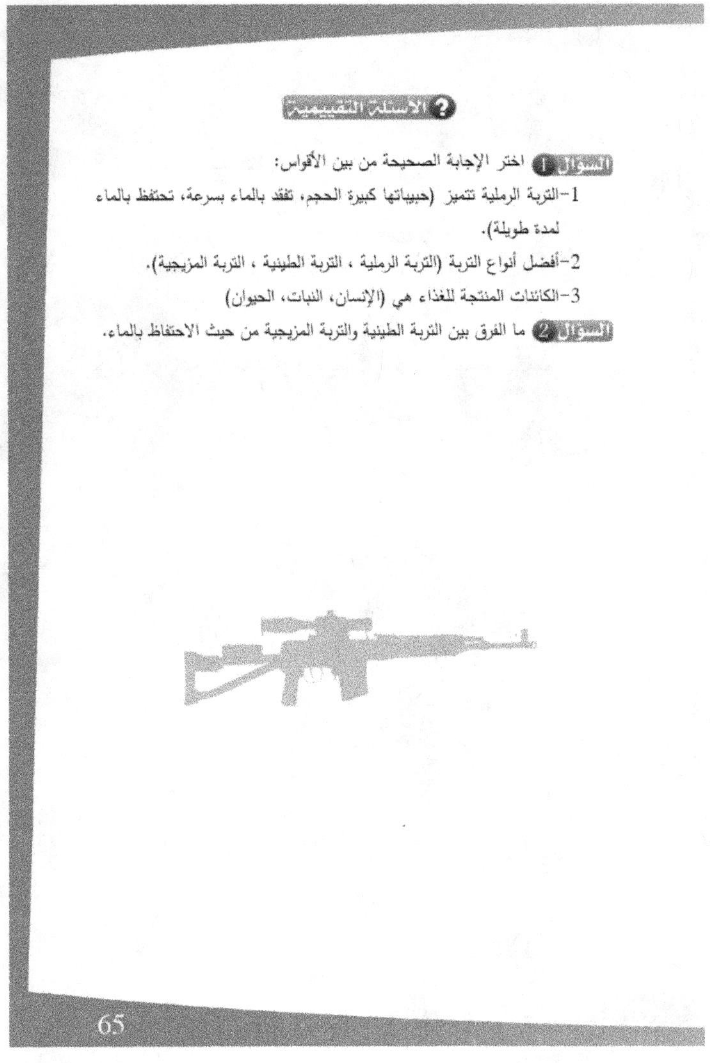

الأسئلة التقييمية

السؤال 1 اختر الإجابة الصحيحة من بين الأقواس:

1-التربة الرملية تتميز (حبيباتها كبيرة الحجم، تفقد بالماء بسرعة، تحتفظ بالماء لمدة طويلة).

2-أفضل أنواع التربة (التربة الرملية ، التربة الطينية ، التربة المزيجية).

3-الكائنات المنتجة للغذاء هي (الإنسان، النبات، الحيوان)

السؤال 2 ما الفرق بين التربة الطينية والتربة المزيجية من حيث الاحتفاظ بالماء.

65

Figure 4.2 (Continued)

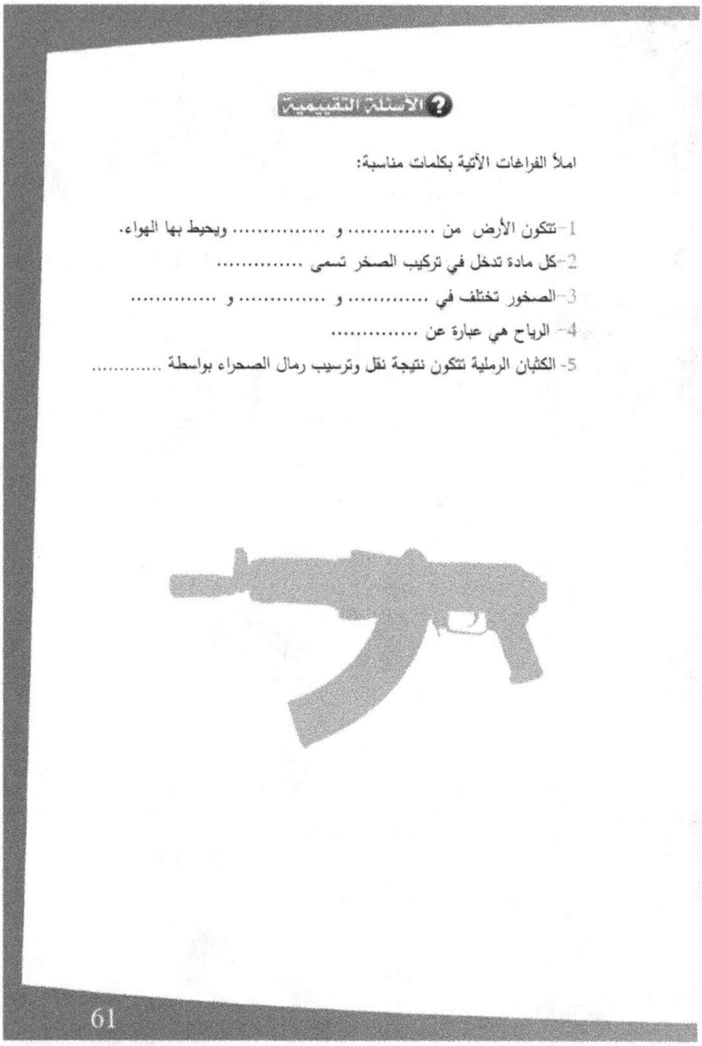

الأسئلة التقييمية

املأ الفراغات الآتية بكلمات مناسبة:

1-تتكون الأرض من .... و .... ويحيط بها الهواء.

2-كل مادة تدخل في تركيب الصخر تسمى ....

3-الصخور تختلف في .... و .... و ....

4- الرياح هي عبارة عن ....

5- الكثبان الرملية تتكون نتيجة نقل وترسيب رمال الصحراء بواسطة ....

61

Figure 4.2 (Continued)

Regarding these educational apps, they can be downloaded anywhere and can work offline, allowing more users from any part of the world to engage with them, which can ultimately enhance ISIS brand image. Second, the apps are fun, interactive, and interesting to use due to their audiovisual content, making them more appealing than using textbooks. Third, the apps project a brand image of the terrorist group that is technologically tech savvy, advanced, and versatile which can be used for promotion.

Further, the results of this chapter show that the educational apps are largely meant to teach standardized and strict Islamic jurisdiction as well as Arabic language which can both assist in creating a jihadist nation-state through standardization. These apps are also meant to militarize or what I term 'jihadize' children using a variety of strategies. In this respect, 'jihadize' means the process of implanting the concept of jihad and promoting it in the minds of new recruits and in the scope of this study, it will be related to children. For example, the 'Letters: Teaching the Alphabet to the Cubs' app (see Figure 4.3) is designed in two parts, both for very young children as it deals with basic Arabic language learning skills, especially the alphabetical letters.

This indicates that these apps are used for private educational purposes mostly targeting kindergarteners. Using the Walkthrough method, there is a link in the app to Al-Bayan radio station, and there is also some background information on Al-Himmah Library, making the app serve multiple purposes. Though not all the examples contain military words and pictures, they still constitute a sizable sample. For example, Figure 4.4 showcases modern weapons when teaching the alphabet, while Figure 4.5 highlights old weaponry. I argue here that the use of old weapons is meant to provide a nostalgic view of the Islamic Caliphate which can invoke positive sentiments among young learners.

The terrorist group planned on managing an imagined state that was allegedly similar to what appeared in early Islam (Thielman, 2014; Shane & Hubbard, 2014), particularly in connection with religious rules, duties, and obligations such as alms giving and praying on time. Hence, many messages in these educational apps emphasize following Islamic teachings religiously. There is also emphasis on highlighting the Islamic Golden Dinar, which is ISIS' standardized currency, giving the perception of a real state. In general, the majority of other audio and visual examples are meant

Figure 4.3 The educational app 'Letters'.

Source: archive.org.

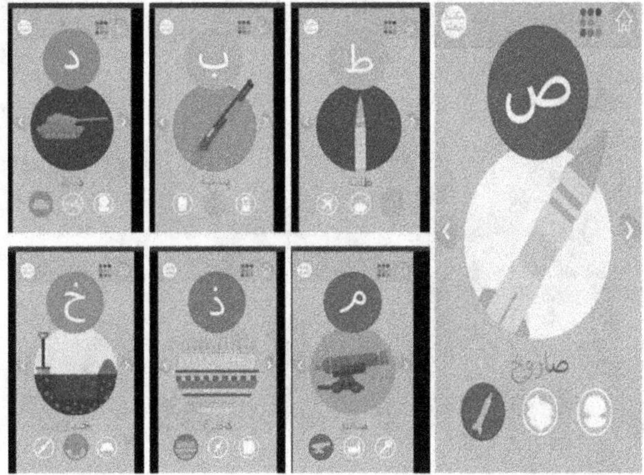

Figure 4.4 Showcasing modern weapons in the 'Letters' app.

Source: archive.org.

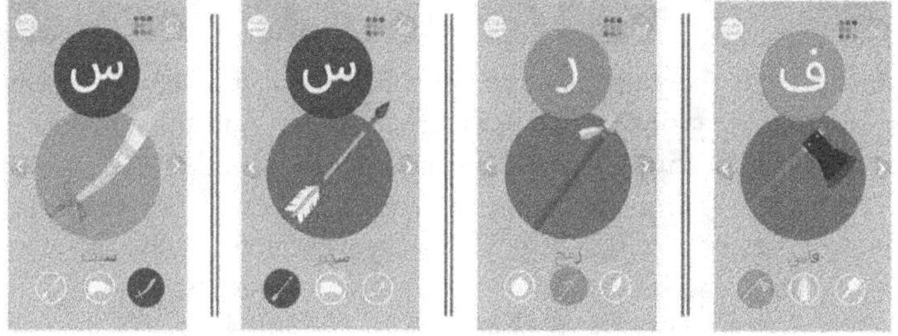

Figure 4.5 Showcasing old weapons in the 'Letters' app.

Source: archive.org.

to enhance strict religious beliefs and the idea of the material existence of ISIS, while the militarization of the curriculum is meant to 'jihadize' the young generation in a way that makes war, fighting, and violence normalized in everyday life.

In relation to the second app 'Night and Day Supplications' (see Figure 4.6), it can be described as a very simple app for young

Figure 4.6 The 'Night and Day Supplication' educational app.

Source: archive.org.

children to learn 42 night- and daytimes Islamic supplications and prayers.

Similar to the previous app, its audiovisual interactive goal is to enhance religious beliefs in an engaging way, and two sections include supplications against the enemy and another one to be recited when facing the enemy and those in power. For example, one supplication states: 'Oh God who revealed thy Book, who speeds the judgement, defeat the opponent parties. God defeat them and destabilize them' (Figure 4.7). Figures 4.7 and 4.8 show the interactive feature of the app as the user needs to click on the weapons to activate them in targeting enemy tanks that carry US flag as well as enemy camps that have the national flags of most coalition forces fighting ISIS. As can be seen, the user attains a simplistic sense of agency and a perceived idea of victory when clicking on the weapons as the tanks, flags, and camp tents get easily destroyed.

Finally, the 'Alphabet Teacher' educational app (see Figure 4.9) is similar to the previous two apps as there is once again emphasis on the militarization of the curriculum and disseminating strict religious beliefs.

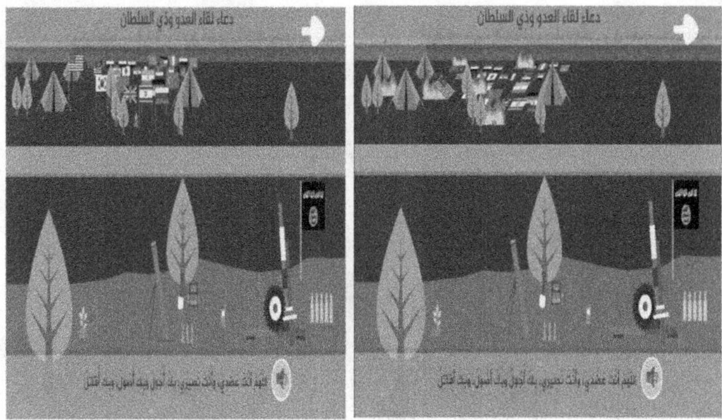

Figure 4.7 Supplication when facing the enemy or those in power in the 'Night and Day Supplication' app.

Source: archive.org.

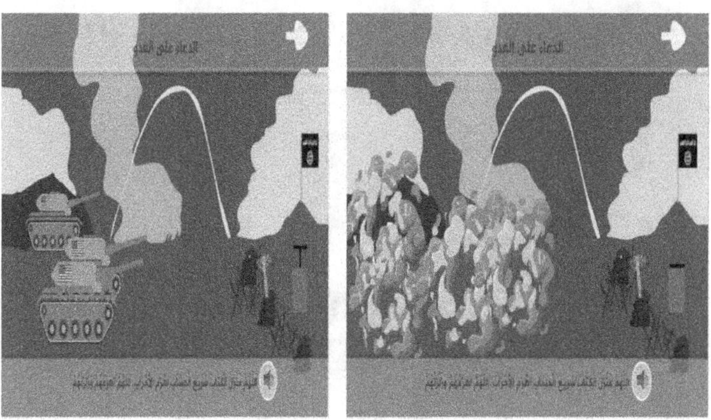

Figure 4.8 Supplication against the enemy in the 'Night and Day Supplication' app.

Source: archive.org.

Figure 4.9 The 'Alphabet Teacher' educational app.

Source: archive.org.

To enhance the belief in ISIS' brand, the app highlights some common statements like 'it will remain by God's willing' in reference to the Islamic State. Similarly, ISIS currency, which is the golden Islamic Dinar, is used to remind the app's users of the perceived legitimacy of the terrorist group. When observing the educational items that are used to teach the Arabic alphabet, we can find that 13 out of 22 ones are militarized to enhance the sense of warfare and conflict among children. In brief, the goals of these educational apps are to enhance militarization, weapon training, jihadist thought, and extremism.

As discussed in Chapter 1, ISIS intended to build a transnational Jihadist Ummah state with the use of media due to its importance in shaping a collective identity. ISIS' goal was to create followers who were actively willing to participate in jihad and blindly follow all of ISIS' rules without questioning their superiors. To educate children on the importance of jihad, ISIS introduced their appealing mobile apps as a means to influence them. This jihadist identity was the ideal that ISIS sought to establish in its imagined Islamist state, and children were the ideal target groups who can be easily mobilized from an early age. In reality, ISIS attempted to use its own radical version of Islam as a unifier to militarize and subsequently *jihadize* younger generations partly via using these educational apps, for they are cultural sites that are also used as a branding strategy to show the terrorist group as technologically advanced.

To sum up, ISIS actively sought to create a state by marketing its global brand as a powerful one partly using media propaganda like its educational apps. In its state-building efforts, mobile communication techniques are used to target children living under ISIS' control. In global marketing, international brands using standardized advertising need to be available to consumers by their high visibility, unified logo, and standard messages (de Mooij, 2010), and ISIS achieved something similar with its use of standardized messages in these educational apps in an attempt to create a stronger brand whether be inside its past territories or outside them.

References

Al-Rawi, A. (2020). Mobile news apps as sites of transnational ethnic mediascapes. *The Journal of International Communication*, *26*(1), 73–91.

Anderson, B. (2006). *Imagined communities: Reflections on the origin and spread of nationalism.* New York: Verso Books.

Appadurai, A. (1990). Disjuncture and difference in the global cultural economy. *Theory, Culture & Society, 7*(2–3), 295–310.

Arvisais, O., Bruyère, M. H., Chamsine, C., & Mahhou, M. A. (2021). The educational intentions of the Islamic State through its textbooks. *International Journal of Educational Development, 87*, 102506.

Arvisais, O., & Guidère, M. (2020). Education in conflict: How Islamic State established its curriculum. *Journal of Curriculum Studies, 52*(4), 498–515.

Berman, E. & Shapiro, J. (2015, November 29). Why ISIL will fail on its own. *Politico Magazine.* Retrieved from www.politico.com/magazine/story/2015/11/why-isil-will-fail-on-its-own-213401

Bhabha, H. (1994). *The location of culture.* London: Routledge.

De Mooij, M. (2010). *Global marketing and advertising: Understanding cultural paradoxes.* Thousand Oaks, CA: Sage Publications, Inc.

Deslandes-Martineau, M., Charland, P., Lapierre, H. G., Arvisais, O., Chamsine, C., Venkatesh, V., & Guidère, M. (2022). The programming curriculum within ISIS. *PLoS One, 17*(4), e0265721.

Gadais, T., Touir, G., Décarpentrie, L., Al-Khatib, M., Daou, A., Chamsine, C., & Arvisais, O. (2022). Education under the Islamic State of Iraq and Syria: A content analysis of the physical education curriculum. *Frontiers in Education. 7*, 854413. doi: 10.3389/feduc.2022.854413

Hassan, H. (2016, June 13). the sectarianism of the Islamic State: Ideological roots and political context. Carnegie Endowment for International Peace. Retrieved from http://carnegieendowment.org/2016/06/13/sectarianism-of-islamic-state-ideological-roots-and-political-context-pub-63746

Light, B., Burgess, J., & Duguay, S. (2018). The walkthrough method: An approach to the study of apps. *New Media & Society, 20*(3), 881–900.

Liptak, K. (2016, February 25). Obama expresses little optimism for Syrian ceasefire. CNN. Retrieved from www.cnn.com/2016/02/25/politics/obama-isis-syria-ceasefire/index.html

Melchior, J. (2014). ISIS tactics illustrate social media's new place in modern war. *TechCrunch.* Retrieved from: http://techcrunch.com/2014/10/15/isis-tactics-illustrate-social-medias-new-place-in-modern-war

Olidort, J. (2016). Inside the Caliphate's classroom: Textbooks, guidance literature, and indoctrination methods of the Islamic State. Washington Institute for Near East Policy. Retrieved from www.washingtoninstitute.org/media/2044?disposition=attachment

Shane, S. & Hubbard, B. (2014, August 30). ISIS displaying a deft command of varied media. *The New York Times*. Retrieved from www.nytimes.com/2014/08/31/world/middleeast/isis-displaying-a-deft-command-of-varied-media.html?partner=rss&emc=rss&smid=tw-nytimes&_r=0

Singer, P. W. (2003). Fighting child soldiers. *Military Review*, *83*(3), 26.

Thielman, S. (2014, September 10). ISIS' sinister media strategy, and how the west is fighting back. *ADWeek*. Retrieved from www.adweek.com/news/television/isiss-sinister-media-strategy-and-how-west-fighting-back-160021

Townsend, M. (2016, March 5). How Islamic State is training child killers in doctrine of hate. *The Guardian*. Retrieved from www.theguardian.com/world/2016/mar/05/islamic-state-trains-purer-child-killers-in-doctrine-of-hate

Urry, J. (2002). Mobility and proximity. *Sociology*, *36*(2), 255–74.

5 The Dark Web*

Introduction

The Dark Web is an integral part of the Internet, but it offers seemingly end-to-end encrypted service. Technically speaking, one needs a special browser to access the Dark Web such as the Onion Router (Tor) I2P, or JonDonym, and it is different from the surface and deep web where most websites are indexed. The surface web is what everyone can access and search using Google or Bing, while the Dark Web refers to websites that are not yet indexed (Ozkaya & Islam, 2019, p. 8) as well as other sites that require special log-in credentials. In other words, the Dark Web is not accessible using the surface web and traditional browsers. In addition, the Dark Web is often used for nefarious purposes such as terrorism (Marius & Ungureanu, 2016; Park et al., 2016), illicit drug sale, and illegal activities like conducting in-demand human experiments, paying for red rooms where torture is administered, selling forged documents, or hiring assassins and hackers (Faizan & Khan, 2019). Most of the financial transactions on the Dark Web occur with the help of cryptocurrencies due to the difficulty of tracing the funds and services exchanged and the people behind

* I am grateful for the funding I received from the Canadian government's Department of Heritage that allowed me to subscribe to this tool to conduct an unrelated research project. The Digital Citizen Contribution Program – Department of Heritage, 2021–2022, 'Understanding hate groups' narratives and conspiracy theories in traditional and alternative social media'. I would like to thank Mr Justin Seitz for his kind assistance in offering me technical guidance and a free Hunchly crawler license.

DOI: 10.4324/9781032615882-6

them. Due to the difficulty of indexing and searching the Dark Web, there is an increasing interest in systematically studying it using a variety of digital tools (Chen, 2012; Popov, Bergman, & Valassi, 2018; Sobhan et al., 2022) and qualitative methods (Gehl, 2018b).

Currently, there is very little empirical research on ISIS' use of the Dark Web. Due to its anonymous nature and relative ease of access, a few researchers have warned and made references to the fact that the terrorist group does 'use the dark web forums to spread the messages to the world and recruit new members to the organization with the violent targets' (Godawatte et al., 2019, pp. 492–493). In this respect, Gabriel Weimann is correct in his characterization of the terrorist group's media presence and his recommendation to further research the Dark Web, for:

> ISIS has not had an official presence on Twitter since July 2014, when its last accounts were shut down. Despite the pressure on its media operation, ISIS has always proved highly resilient and adaptable: it started experimenting with a series of less well-known social media platforms, such as the privacy-focused Diaspora as well as VKontakte...
>
> (2016, p. 202)

One of the few available studies on the use of the Dark Web by Salafi jihadists was conducted by Lakomy (2023). The author identified seven onion domains that were active between 2020 and 2022 and offered a descriptive overview of their infrastructure. The study included sites that belonged to Al-Qaeda, the Taliban, and ISIS; however, there was no in-depth analysis of these Dark Web sites' content. Instead, there are only short descriptions of the sites' sections. In brief, this chapter fills a major gap in the literature because it systematically analyzes ISIS' most recent propaganda content on the Dark Web using a mixed-method approach. The terrorist group uses the Dark Web to project an imagined nation-state notion in the sense that it is still actively strong and has centralized power over several regions around Africa and the Middle East using standardized media productions.

Methodologically, I first identified ISIS' official Dark Web site, i3lam (media), by searching in the commercial tool Echosec

Systems – Beacon in late 2021 for the Arabic word 'باقية' (remaining) which is one of ISIS' slogans. This slogan suggests that the state will allegedly remain in existence forever, and I found it useful in identifying ISIS' materials because of its unique meaning. At that time, the i3lam Dark Website had a replica on the surface web with a similar name; however, it was deleted about a year later. Three other ISIS-related nonofficial Dark Websites were subsequently identified by using the surface web, especially when searching the Archive.org website since one site referred to the other including AlRaud (Thunders), Fihrras An-Insar (The Supporters' Archive), and Akhbar Al-Muslimeen (Muslims' news). These three sites disseminated reports mostly in Arabic, English, and French which were all taken from the i3lam website. The latter site, however, offered updated news in 21 different languages and contained links to 5,823 reports dating back to July 14, 2014.

This official site has subsections to cover the different *willayats* (provinces) in which ISIS is active, and I focused on Arabic news reports because they are more comprehensive than other languages. For example, as of July 11, 2023, the Khalifaha News subsection contained 339 pages in Arabic, though its English section contained slightly more (n = 344) due to the fact that it is mixed with Al Nabaa's newspaper infographics as well as the press releases of ISIS' media branches in different parts of the world. The Arabic version of the website was more organized in terms of the distribution of news based on the *willayats.* All of the above four Dark Web sites are often daily updated with propaganda, and they contain almost all of ISIS' multimedia news repositories dating back to several years ago.

To access the above four Dark Websites, I used the Tor Browser and a VPN tool, and to retrieve the data, I used the Hunchly crawler that can be customized on the Chrome browser when using the Dark Web. There was a need to customize the tool because 'the large base of research work on surface Web is inapplicable to the deep Web due to differences in using basic building blocks of the Webpages and links' (Kaczmarek & Węckowski, 2014, p. 176). Crawling the Dark Web for content is an established data collection method used in previous studies (Chen, 2012, pp. 49–50). According to Robert Gehl, there are three main routes in studying the Dark Web, including 'participant observation, digital archives, and the experience of running the routing software required to access the Dark Web' (2018a, p. 31). I mostly used the second method which is related to building a digital archive on my personal PC for further analysis. Though I did not engage with any ISIS members or participate in commenting or posting materials, I did conduct regular observations of the website which is similar to online fieldwork or virtual ethnography (see Sidoti, 2022). This was important to monitor the online discussion and document any website updates.

The size of the collected data set from Hunchly exceeded 1.4 GB, comprising 2,223 images associated with news as well as all textual content including the headline and lead. I then extracted the textual content from all the downloaded PDF files in order to conduct topic modeling that utilizes factor analysis. These topics are ranked according to their dominance in the data set and are based on their eigenvalue scores, using QDA Miner 6–Word Stat 9 (for more details, see Al-Rawi, 2017; Al-Rawi, Ackah, & Chun, 2023). Using Proximity Plot and Link Analysis, I identified some relevant words and their associations with other terms. I also used other ISIS-affiliated Dark Websites. For example, the Al Muslimeen News Dark Website contains an archive of all their posted materials which consist of 7,236 headlines and their associated links arranged in a structured way. The collected data set was analyzed for further textual analysis and visualized chronologically based on the frequency of referencing the different territories. As for the AlRaud Media Archive Dark Website, it contained 140 comments from ISIS sympathizers and supporters as of July 10, 2023. I checked the comments after 15 days, and four more posts had been added, suggesting that there was ongoing activity and engagement from other users. Then, I conducted a critical document reading of these comments to carefully analyze the corpus. Based on critical theory, this is a qualitative method that requires an in-depth analysis of the collected data. I also used a digital method to extract the most common phrases used in these comments. Finally, I conducted a qualitative thematic analysis and classification of the collected news images using grounded theory, similar to the method I followed in classifying ISIS' propaganda billboard.

Findings

I will first begin the discussion of the results with the terrorist group's online presence on other sites that are advertised on the Dark Web. Ironically, if one searches Archive.org for the word 'i3lam', which is the group's official media outlet, one can find references to the Dark Website link and other replicas on the surface web as of July 2023.

For example, the website Obedient Supporters (https://obedientsupporters.co/) offers followers the means to download all of ISIS' propaganda materials and the ability to receive updated news via Telegram. There are references to numerous other websites active on the surface web; however, they often are deleted after a short period of time. As I monitored their online presence, I found that most of them were deleted when I last checked in June and July 2023, including: https://fahras.eth.limo, https://fahras.re, https://alfaj.re/public/alfajr, https://alraud.link/?p=29573, and https://ilnews.co. Other popular channels that are found on Telegram include 'Tamkin News Agency' (https://t.me/tm1443kin), which is referenced eight times in i3lam's news reports, and 'Nashir News Agency' (https://t.me/vv1144), which is mentioned six times on the same Dark Website. Several other Telegram channels are identified, including bots that can be activated when pressing the 'Start' button. When one Telegram channel is deleted, a few other ones emerge, allowing interested users to stay connected and to download all of ISIS' media materials including several GBs of data.[1] On one of ISIS' Dark Websites, there is even a link to a Google sheet where one can enter their contact details and receive private messages. I argue here that the use of Telegram bots and this Google sheet is meant to personalize the experience of connecting with ISIS, offering the terrorist group an effective means to collect personal data from other users. In addition, QR codes are often provided to offer Tor users ease of access in case they lose the hyperlinks or forget to bookmark them. In brief, ISIS is increasingly using non-US-based platforms and sites in order to remain active online for longer periods of time, but the main source of information and its most stable one remains the Dark Web.

In terms of the monthly frequency of ISIS' media posts, the results show that December 2015 witnessed the highest number of news reports (*n* = 455) followed by November of the same year (*n* = 420) and January 2016 (*n* = 360). As for the annual distribution of news reports, the year 2015 witnessed the highest number of posts (*n* = 3,101) followed by the year 2016 (*n* = 1,380), closely corresponding with the group's offline activities and control over large areas and territories (Figure 5.1).

As can be seen from the top figure, the same year also witnessed the highest number of posts per day (*n* = 26). In general though,

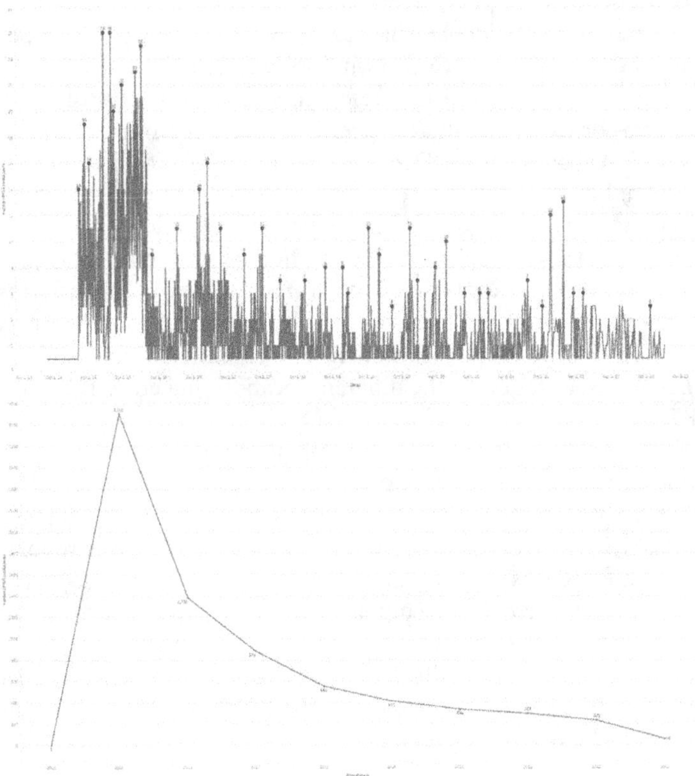

Figure 5.1 Distribution of ISIS's daily (top) and annual (bottom) posts.

Source: Author's creation.

starting from 2016, ISIS' news reports have witnessed a gradual decline trend, clearly echoing the organization's increased weakness. The largest decrease happened in 2017 and 2018 following the Coalition-led attacks on the terrorist group.

In terms of its current activities, most of ISIS' media discussion and offline presence seem to be focused on West Africa. In this respect and to better examine the changes in ISIS activities throughout the previous years, I extracted references to over 30 different *willayats* (territories or regions) that witnessed some ISIS terrorist operations. As shown in Figure 5.2, most of the current, most intense, and ongoing ISIS terrorist activities can be found in Africa, with a focus on Nigeria and a few other neighboring countries.

There is also evidence that some Egyptian territories, especially the Sinai Desert, are also witnessing increasing activities. On the other hand, we find that references to ISIS' previously held locations or focus of military operations, such as Nineveh, Mosul, Aleppo, Anbar, Salah Al-Deen, and Damascus, were much more frequent before 2017. If we examine the overall references to these locations using a Proximity Plot which statistically measures the strength of these associations, we will find, as shown in Table 5.1, the co-occurrences of the word *Willaya* in Arabic with other terms denoting geographical locations. In this respect, Nineveh comes first followed by Aleppo and Sinai. Figure 5.3 also offers a Link Analysis visualization of the different locations linked to the word *Willaya*.

To better understand the overall discussion, I conducted a topic modeling analysis of ISIS' news reports' headlines. The most dominant topic is 'News of the Islamic State' (eigenvalue: 5.87), which is expected since almost all the news reports contain references to this expression, but the associated keywords suggest that there is an emphasis on the words 'fighters' and 'attack', suggesting that the majority of news reports and propaganda are related to the alleged military operations of the terrorist group. The second most dominant topic is 'Sinai Willaya (eigenvalue: 4.41) and the Egyptian Army', indicating ISIS' increasing operations in this region. The associated keywords include terms such as 'explosive device', 'bombing', and 'apostate' in relation to the Egyptian Army, while specific locations are often used like Al Arish city, Al Abid well, and Sheikh Zuweid. The third topic

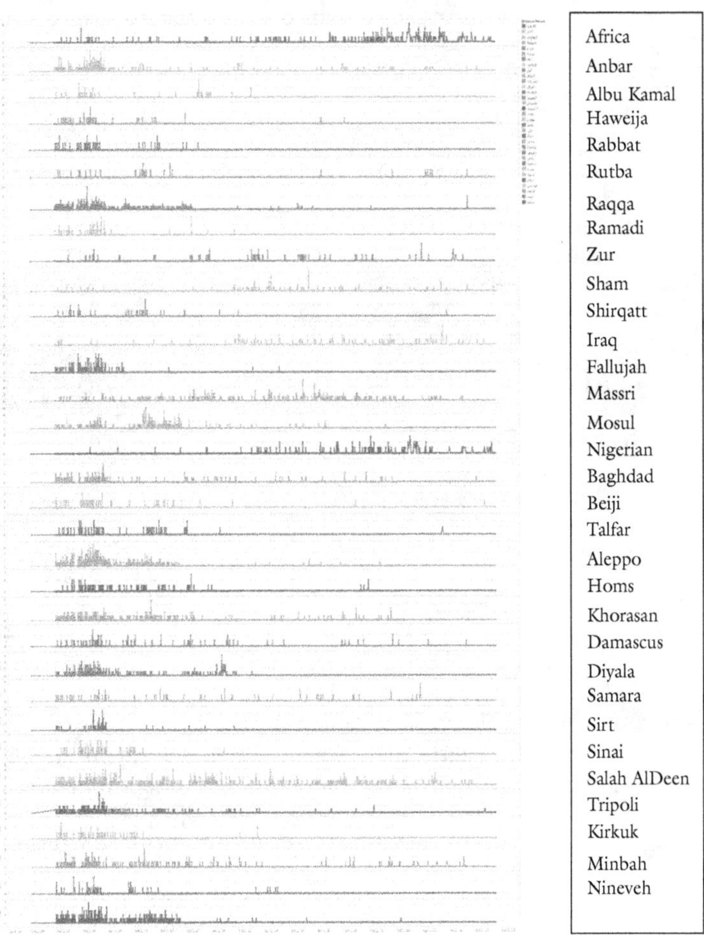

Figure 5.2 A longitudinal distribution of references to ISIS's *willayat*.

Note: Text box on the right is a translation of the Arabic locations of this figure.

Source: Author's creation.

Table 5.1 Co-occurrences of the word *Willaya* with other territories

No.	*Keyword*	*Co-occurrences*	*Association*
1.	(Nineveh) نينوى	385	0.082
2.	(Aleppo) حلب	417	0.080
3.	(Sinai) سيناء	384	0.069
4.	(Salah [Al-Deen]) صلاح	224	0.047
5.	(Anbar) الأنبار	227	0.044
6.	(Jazeera) الجزيرة	204	0.044
7.	(Africa) إفريقية	193	0.041
8.	(Homs) حمص	203	0.037
9.	(Raqqa) الرقة	238	0.032
10.	(Damascus) دمشق	201	0.031
11.	(Kirkuk) كركوك	161	0.028
12.	(Sham) الشام	103	0.022
13.	(Iraq) العراق	97	0.019
14.	(Mosul) الموصل	151	0.017
15.	(Khorasan) خراسان	79	0.017
16.	(Fallujah) الفلوجة	98	0.016
17.	(Hama) حماة	83	0.016
18.	(Baghdad) بغداد	100	0.016
19.	(Tripoli) طرابلس	64	0.013
20.	(Ramadi) الرمادي	63	0.012

is 'Islamic State's soldiers in Africa' (eigenvalue: 4.07), and there is a clear focus on Nigeria and its army which is always described as 'apostate', similar to the Egyptian Army. The only sub-location associated with this topic is the Bornu region in Nigeria. The fourth topic is the 'Crusading Coalition Bombardment' (eigenvalue: 3.46) and the word 'Safavid' which is a reference to Shiites strongly associated with this topic, implying a religious alliance between Christians and Shiites has been established to fight against Sunnis. Other associated words include 'Russian bombardment', 'destruction', and 'Muslim people', clearly indicating the Syrian context of this topic and highlighting the human impact of the Russian military operations. The last two topics include 'Salah Al-Deen Willaya' (eigenvalue: 3.22) focusing on ISIS' military operations in Samara and Beiji, and 'Allah accept him in Heaven' (eigenvalue: 3.06) in reference to the killing of

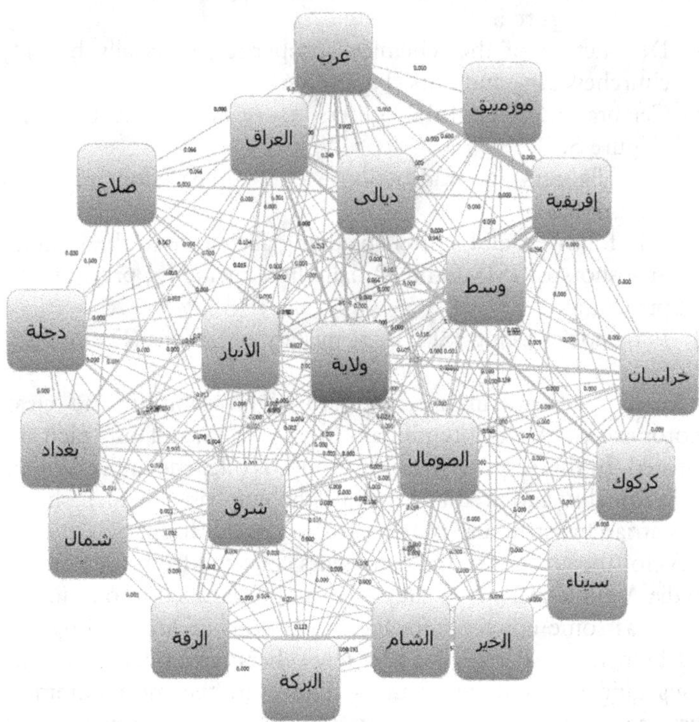

Figure 5.3 Link analysis of the word *Willaya* and its association with different territories.

Source: Author's creation.

ISIS' leader, Abu Ibrahim Al Qurashi Al Baghdadi (Table 5.2) in February 2022.

As for the news images associated with the news reports, the qualitative thematic analysis suggests they broadly fall into nine main themes:

(1) Executed or about to be executed as well as dead and beheaded enemies and prisoners (Figure 5.4).
(2) Captured prisoners who are still alive.

(3) War trophies including weaponry or captured property such as cars (Figure 5.5).
(4) Destruction of the 'enemies'' properties, especially houses, churches, cars, and huts (Figure 5.6).
(5) Celebrating fallen ISIS fighters, especially suicide bombers (Figure 5.7).
(6) ISIS fighters in war action or in preparation to fight (Figure 5.8).
(7) ISIS followers and fighters pledging allegiance to the Caliph.
(8) Snapshots of ISIS fighters' daily lives including praying and preaching.
(9) Infographics listing ISIS' latest military operations (Figure 5.9).

In all the news images, we find high-resolution and clear photos except for the intentionally blurred faces, and only men are featured. In this respect, these clear photos offer the impression of professionality and credibility, while the emphasis on men shows the patriarchal structure of the terrorist organization.

As for the analysis of the comments collected from the AlRaud Media Archive Dark Web site, they can be classified into different topics, as some commenters asked questions in Arabic, English, and French on Sharia law and a few others responded with religious guidance and instructions. However, the most common phrases include 'Crypto currency' (n = 5), 'Allah bestow victory' (n = 5), 'Monero crypto' (n = 5), 'Your children' (in English) (n = 4), and 'Islamic state' (n = 4). As many users asked about how they could support jihad, the common answer was through 'donating money' to ISIS via cryptocurrencies. In this respect, the i3lam and AlRaud Dark Websites include their Monero cryptocurrency (XMR) wallet numbers to allow ISIS sympathizers to pay directly. Monero is used because of the privacy it affords unlike other cryptocurrencies. In the comments section, we further find detailed instructions on how to create an account with Monero and send money. There is also guidance on online privacy and the need to use the Numero app which is a virtual phone number that helps in creating a fake number. The latter seems to assist in creating a Telegram account instead of using one's real phone number that can be easily traced. To give an example, one user gave the following long and detailed advice in French

Table 5.2 Topic modeling of ISIS' news headline reports

No.	*Topic*	*Keywords*	*Coherence (NPMI)*	*Eigenvalue*
1.	اخبار الدولة الإسلامية	الدولة; الإسلامية; أعماق; وكالة; مقاتلي; الزور; دير; لمقاتلي; مقتل; مقاتلو; الدولة الإسلامية; وكالة أعماق; مقاتلي الدولة الإسلامية; لمقاتلي الدولة الإسلامية; مقاتلو الدولة الإسلامية; دير الزور; مقتل وإصابة; هجوم لمقاتلي الدولة الإسلامية;	0.368	5.87
2.	ولاية سيناءوالجيش المصري	ناسفة; عبوة; المصري; سيناء; بتفجير; زويد; بسيناء; رفح; تفجير; أمس; آلية; وإصابة; أدى; الشيخ; العريش; جنوب; للجيش; المرتد; حاجز; ولاية سيناء; للجيش المصري; عبوة ناسفة; المصري المرتد; الجيش المصري; الشيخ زويد; للجيش المصري المرتد; جنوب مدينة; الجيش المصري المرتد; تفجير عبوة ناسفة; بتفجير عبوة ناسفة; مدينة العريش; لجيش الردة; أول أمس; هلاك وإصابة; الردة المصري; بتفجير مقاتلي الدولة الإسلامية; وإصابة من كان على متنها; شمال سيناء; بئر العبد; بعبوة ناسفة	0.402	4.41
3.	جنود الخلافة في إفريقية	إفريقية; الخلافة; برنو; النيجيري; بمنطقة; جنود; نتائج; هجوم; غرب; المرتد; بلدة; للجيش; جنود الخلافة; ولاية غرب; ولاية غرب إفريقية; هجوم جنود الخلافة; رباط جنود الخلافة; لجنود الخلافة; جانب من هجوم جنود الخلافة; للجيش النيجيري; الجيش النيجيري; نتائج هجوم جنود الخلافة; جانب من نتائج; ولاية وسط إفريقية; للجيش النيجيري المرتد; الخلافة على ثكنات; ثكنة للجيش;	0.456	4.07

(*Continued*)

Table 5.2 (Continued)

No.	*Topic*	*Keywords*	*Coherence (NPMI)*	*Eigenvalue*
4.	قصف التحالف الصليبي	;الصليبي; قصف; التحالف; آثار; طيران; المسلمين; الصفوي; عوام التحالف الصليبي; الصليبي الصفوي; طيران التحالف الصليبي; آثار قصف; التحالف الصليبي النصيري; قصف التحالف الصليبي; التحالف الصليبي الصفوي; قصف طيران التحالف الصليبي; آثار الدمار; عوام المسلمين; قصف الطيران; آثار القصف; المسلمين في مدينة; طيران التحالف الصليبي النصيري; آثار القصف الصليبي الصفوي; الجيش الصفوي; قصف التحالف الصليبي النصيري; آثار الدمار الذي خلفه قصف; آثار قصف الطيران; التحالف الصليبي الصفوي على مدينة; قصف الطيران الروسي; قصف طائرات التحالف; آثار قصف التحالف الصليبي; عوام المسلمين في مدينة; ;قصف طيران التحالف الصليبي النصيري	0.360	3.46
5.	ولاية صلاح الدين	صلاح; الدين; سامراء; الر; الهاون; بيجي; ثكنات; شمال; الجيش; ;بقذائف صلاح الدين; ولاية صلاح الدين; غرب مدينة سامراء; الجيش الصفوي; شمال بغداد; مدينة بيجي; ولاية شمال بغداد; غرب مدينة; ثكنات الجيش; الجيش; غرب مدينة بيجي; الخلافة على ثكنات; ;بقذائف الهاون; سدة سامراء; الجيش الصفوي وميليشياته	0.286	3.22
6.	تقبله الله الشيخ أمير المؤمنين	;أبي; حفظه; الله; تعالى; الشيخ; المؤمنين; مؤسسة; تقبله تقبله الله; الله تعالى; حفظه الله; الشيخ أبي; الشيخ المجاهد أبي; مؤسسة الفرقان; حفظه الله تعالى; كلمة صوتية; أبي إبراهيم; الهاشمي القرشي; معسكر الشيخ أبي; بتوفيق الله تعالى; بيعة جنود الخلافة لأمير المؤمنين; أبي الحسن; أبي بكر; غزوة الشيخ أبي; أبي عمر; القرشي البغدادي; غزوة أبي; للدولة الإسلامية الشيخ المجاهد أبي; ;تقدم كلمة صوتية للمتحدث الرسمي	0.350	3.06

Figure 5.4 Theme 1: About to be executed ISIS prisoners.

Note: Two alleged Iraqis who are labeled as 'spies for the Rafidhi Army' in Ramadi (top) and Riadh (bottom) about to be executed.

Source: Dark Web.

and English on how to use cryptocurrency and maintain online privacy:

> Assallam alaykum siblings, please do not use crypto exchanges and services that have kyc. What is kyc? Kyc means knowing your customer, these are used by a multitude of companies to

Figure 5.5 Theme 2: War trophies like weaponry or captured property.

Note: Alleged war trophies taken from the Cameroonian Army (top) and Nigerian army (bottom).

Source: Dark Web.

prevent "illegal" activities from happening, exchanges such as coinbase and others require information about you, so if you try to donate to muwahid, they will know exactly who you are and where you live, if you want a complete list of services that don't have kyc, visit the website "kycnot. me", just remove the space between "." and "me". The site recommends you to use the

Figure 5.6 Theme 3: Destruction of the 'enemies'' properties, especially houses, churches, cars, and huts.

Note: Alleged destruction of army properties in Nigeria (top) and its allied militias (bottom).

Source: Dark Web.

exchange known as bisq, there are many guides on how to set it up and fund it on youtube. Another recommendation is to use a virtual machine. What is a virtual machine? A virtual machine is basically another system running on your system. You can find many tutorials on youtube on how to set this up if you have a Windows machine, I recommend using Virtual Box and Kali

Figure 5.7 Theme 4: Celebrating fallen ISIS fighters, especially suicide bombers.

Note: Images from West Africa allegedly showing Omar Al-Insari (top) and Abu Othman Al-Insari (bottom) before conducting their suicide attacks.

Source: Dark Web.

Linux for easy use, but if you are good with computers, you can make Kali your main operating system instead of the spyware filth known as Windows and if you can't give up Windows for some reason, buy a separate laptop (it doesn't have to be expensive as long as it can do the job) and completely remove Windows and install fresh Kali Linux on the drive (i e bare

Figure 5.8 Theme 5: ISIS fighters in war action or in preparation to fight.

Note: Alleged ISIS military operations in Niger (top) and Ituri Province in Congo (bottom).

Source: Dark Web.

metal) or If you have no money to spend, you can also install kali linux on a spare flash drive and it does not save data when ejected, which could be an advantage or a disadvantage. Tip 1 don't tell anyone about this laptop/computer/flash drive, Tip 2 don't connect this laptop to your home network unless you know how to route traffic through the network tor again many

Figure 5.9 Theme 9: Infographics listing ISIS's latest military operations.

Note: ISIS operations allegedly conducted from June 29, 2023 to July 5, 2023 in the different *willayats* including West Africa (n = 24), Mozambique (n = 18), Sham (Syria) (n = 4), Khurasan (n = 2), and Iraq (n = 2).

Source: Dark Web.

> online guides on setup, Tip 3 secure this laptop/flash drive in a safe place because you don't know who's watching. So, to conclude that modern problems require modern solutions, you have to stay one step ahead of these dirty disbelievers because they don't want to see Islam flourish.

As mentioned above, many commentators expressed interest in supporting and/or joining jihad. However, the main response revolves around financial aid since 'war is fought on all fronts', as one user stressed. There is also clear caution exercised, as one user stated the following in English in May 2023: 'Salam alaikum. I need recruiter i am American and support the state Alhamdulillah'. Responding to the above comment, another user emphasized the following: 'Dont trust anyone online. Most people are spies. There is no recruitment online. Anyone who says he is a recruiter is a spy'.

In addition, feedback on ISIS' media presence is often shared. For example, one user mentioned in March 2023 that the ALRaud website has 'great impact' and expressed the need to increase ISIS' media activities because the 'war in the virtual world should not be less fierce than that in the field'. Another user said the following '💪 انشرو الروابط حتى ولو لأعداكم' (disseminate the hyperlinks even to your enemies) to which a third user agreed, stating the following:

> ☆☆☆☆☆☆☆☆☆☆☆☆☆☆☆☆☆☆☆☆☆☆
> صحيح مليار بالمئة بل إن الذي جعلني اتعرف على الدولة الإسلامية هو أن اخ مناصر قام بوضع رابط موقع العقاب في أحد فيديوهات اليوتيوب !! نعم لو لم يضع ذلك المناصر الرابط لما علمت ما هي هذا الدولة أعزها الله !!!
> ☆☆☆☆☆☆☆☆☆☆☆☆☆☆☆☆☆☆☆☆☆
>
> (This is a billion times correct! What introduced me to the Islamic State is that a supporting brother pasted a link to Uqab website [ISIS-affiliated] in a YouTube video!! Without that link, I would never have known what this state is about, Allah preserves it!!!)

Finally, another commentator complained in French and English about living in the West due to the need to pay taxes that are allegedly used to fund 'the war led by the crusader coalition against the islamic state' and 'LGBT and sodomism and homosexuality propaganda'. The user emphasized the need to protect

Muslim children from what they termed as 'immoral' propaganda, urging Muslims to 'Help the Islamic state, emigrate and unite the ummah'. In brief, the comments section of the AlRaud Dark Website has created a forum-like site for ISIS sympathizers on which they exchange ideas, advice, propaganda, and guidance on how to maintain online privacy. More concerning, it has become a secure means to explore effective and detailed ways to provide financial support to ISIS, especially through Monero cryptocurrency.

To conclude, the Dark Web has provided ISIS with a stable and secure means to communicate its propaganda messages to a global audience since the i3lam Dark Website alone offers over 20 languages, clearly suggesting the high amount of resources and financial support the terrorist group currently receives. The Dark Web offers the terrorist group the means to brand itself as a borderless nation-state through standardized media productions. I argue here that the i3lam Dark Website functions like an international news organization disseminating its breaking news and updated activities to an international audience, while at the same time attracting attention and gathering financial support with the use of other Dark Websites and media sites, especially Telegram, where the communication becomes more personal and direct. Much more research is needed to examine the magnitude of the Dark Web's links to other platforms and mobile apps such as Telegram, the amounts and sources of cryptocurrency funding ISIS receives, and the nature of users interacting with the terrorist group on the Dark Web. Based on the findings of this chapter, most of ISIS' current military activities and media attention focus on West Africa and the Sinai Desert following their losses in Syria and Iraq.

Note

1 I identified many other Telegram channels and bots, some of which are still active as of July 2023, including 'Nashir News Agency' (https://t.me/bn65789), 'Anbaa News Agency' (https://t.me/drygeedf88), 'Mu'ta News Agency' (https://t.me/Mota_support), 'Sarh Al-Khilafah' (https://t.me/DT_KZPBFBOT), 'Ansar Production' (https://t.me/intaj_subscrb_bot), and 'Obedient Supporters' (https://t.me/obedientsupporters_archivebot).

References

Al-Rawi, A. (2017). Online political activism in Syria: Sentiment analysis of social media. *SAGE Research Studies Cases Part 1.* 1–25. https://doi.org/10.4135/9781473994829

Al-Rawi, A., Ackah, B. B., & Chun, W. H. (2023). The intersectionality of Twitter responses to Black Canadian politicians. *Social Media + Society*, *9*(1), 20563051231157290. http://dx.doi.org/10.1177/20563051231157290

Chen, H. (2012). *Dark web: Exploring and mining the dark side of the web.* In F. Domenach, D. I. Ignatov, & J. Poelmans (Eds.), *Formal concept analysis. ICFCA 2012.* Lecture Notes in Computer Science, 7278. Springer. https://doi.org/10.1007/978-3-642-29892-9_1Springer

Faizan, M., & Khan, R. A. (2019). Exploring and analyzing the dark Web: A new alchemy. *First Monday.* https://doi.org/10.5210/fm.v24i5.9473

Gehl, R. W. (2018a). Archives for the dark web: A field guide for study. In Tai Neilson & David Rheams (Eds.), *Research methods for the digital humanities* (pp. 31–51). Springer.

Gehl, R. W. (2018b). *Weaving the dark web: Legitimacy on Freenet, Tor, and I2P.* MIT Press.

Godawatte, K., Raza, M., Murtaza, M., & Saeed, A. (2019, December). Dark web along with the dark web marketing and surveillance. In *2019 20th International conference on parallel and distributed computing, applications and technologies (PDCAT)* (pp. 483–85). IEEE.

Kaczmarek, T., & Węckowski, D. G. (2014). Harvesting deep web data through producer involvement. In *The Dark Web: Breakthroughs in research and practice* (pp. 175–98). IGI Global.

Lakomy, M. (2023). Dark web jihad: Exploring the militant Islamist information ecosystem on the Onion Router. *Behavioral Sciences of Terrorism and Political Aggression*, 1–20. http://dx.doi.org/10.1080/19434472.2022.2164326

Marius, A., & Ungureanu, C. (2016). The hidden web and the connection with terrorism. *Eur. J. Pub. Ord. & Nat'l Sec.*, 29, 29–32.

Ozkaya, E., & Islam, R. (2019). *Inside the Dark Web.* CRC Press.

Park, A. J., Beck, B., Fletcher, D., Lam, P., & Tsang, H. H. (2016, August). Temporal analysis of radical dark web forum users. In *2016 IEEE/ACM International conference on advances in social networks analysis and mining (ASONAM)* (pp. 880–83). IEEE. https://doi.org/10.1109%2fASONAM.2016.7752341

Popov, O., Bergman, J., & Valassi, C. (2018, November). A framework for a forensically sound harvesting the dark web. In *Proceedings of the Central European cybersecurity conference 2018* (pp. 1–7). https://doi.org/10.1145/3277570.3277584

Sidoti, C. (2022). Smart researching in criminology: Virtual ethnography at the edge. In *Qualitative research in criminology: Cutting-edge methods* (pp. 53–67). Springer. https://hdl.handle.net/10807/230992

Sobhan, S., Williams, T., Faruk, M. J. H., Rodriguez, J., Tasnim, M., Mathew, E., ... & Shahriar, H. (2022, June). A review of Dark Web: Trends and future directions. In *2022 IEEE 46th Annual computers, software, and applications conference (COMPSAC)* (pp. 1780–85). IEEE. https://par.nsf.gov/servlets/purl/10347029

Weimann, G. (2016). Going dark: Terrorism on the dark web. *Studies in Conflict & Terrorism*, *39*(3), 195–206. https://psycnet.apa.org/doi/10.1080/1057610X.2015.1119546

Conclusion

This book deals with the different and under-researched case studies, media strategies, sites, and types of propaganda content distributed by ISIS. The discussion is situated within the concept of propaganda and the manner in which the notion of jihad is utilized by ISIS that falsely brands itself as the alleged protector of Islam and Sunni Muslims. Ironically, ISIS directly and indirectly caused great infrastructural damage in its previously held Sunni-dominated areas, such as Mosul, and was responsible for the killing and disappearance of thousands of Sunnis in its attempts to impose its extremist ideology on the population. To create its false and self-proclaimed state, ISIS followed standardized nation-state building practices, and centralized media productions helped in this process. Yet, this group has never been a real state as it has remained, for most of its existence, virtual in an imagined concept.

Chapter 1 of this book explored the use of standard billboards and other offline publications in ISIS' previously held territories. I argued that these standardized media productions helped in disseminating ISIS' propaganda and militant ideology, especially in relation to imposing its strict social rules and projecting a perceived image of a jihadist nation-state.

Chapter 2 examined the spread of jihadist propaganda via Twitter by ISIS sympathizers and followers using a very large data set collected in early 2017 around the time the terrorist group's posts were systematically removed from traditional social media sites. Through non-centralized information operations, we can see a networked attack around certain issues, especially in Arabic language tweets that mostly focused on demeaning Al-Qaeda and

DOI: 10.4324/9781032615882-7

its leading figures. At that time, Twitter did not seem to be very interested or highly invested in moderating Arabic tweets, and the terrorist group seems to have migrated to other sites such as Telegram and the Dark Web, as a follow-up examination of an anti-US slogan on Twitter revealed the absence of active users who publicly expressed antagonism toward the United States.

Chapter 3 discussed ISIS' video game 'Salil al-Sawarem' (The Clanging of the Swords) and investigated the audience's reactions to it using their YouTube comments. I argued that although the game was not produced by the group's centralized media apparatus, it was used for propaganda to attract the attention of younger people. The findings show that the terrorist group's sympathizers used a 'troll, flame, and engage' approach to silence any of ISIS' critics and possibly attract potential followers. Though most of the YouTube comments were critical of ISIS' game, a few sympathizers highlighted the sectarian aspect to falsely justify ISIS' exclusionary and genocidal policies.

Chapter 4 examined another aspect of ISIS' standardized propaganda that could help in nation-state building efforts by analyzing the group's targeting of children via standardized educational mobile apps. Disguised as offering basic language and religious teaching, the goal behind creating these Arabic apps revolves around shaping children's beliefs on the need to follow militant jihad and ISIS' strict ideology.

Chapter 5 offered a systematic analysis of ISIS' Dark Web sites that are often updated on a daily basis to spread violent propaganda. I argued that the Dark Web remains the most stable site that the terrorist group currently uses because of the difficulty of finding such sites, the anonymity that the Tor browser provides, and the effort it takes to take down ISIS' content. Similar to the billboards and apps, the Dark Web media productions are standardized and help the terrorist group in projecting its brand image of a state to a global audience. ISIS' outreach here is much wider because their official site, i3lam, offers updated news in over 20 languages, making the site function like an international news agency. Other alternative sites such as Telegram bots draw their content from the Dark Web to be distributed to more people, making the communication increasingly personal and encrypted. The results show that ISIS' most recent activities and propaganda are focused on

West Africa, especially Nigeria, and military operations are routinely celebrated and announced as victories.

Recent academic literature on ISIS mostly discusses the terrorist group's military defeats and its previous English language publications. Currently, there is a clear lack of ISIS' online presence if one considers the surface web, but I argued that the group is still very active on the Dark Web where it is harder to track users or even identify these online sites. The Dark Web also offers the terrorist group the means to attract sympathizers, collect donations via Monero cryptocurrency, and disseminate its news updates on a daily basis in more than 20 languages. In particular, one Dark Web site seems to be used as a standardized media site where a few other Dark Web sites obtained their updated news. Using a mixed-method approach, I systematically analyzed ISIS' Dark Web content, which is highly under-researched, in order to identify the strategies used to gain support and the territories where this group is active, as well as to analyze the topics they discuss, the associated news images, and the sympathizers' comments.

In terms of solutions, some observers suggested the total blocking of ISIS' access to the Internet by removing their Twitter accounts and Facebook pages as part of the continuous efforts to wipe out the organization online (Greenberg, 2015; Calamur, 2016). For example, Facebook once claimed in 2017 that it used artificial intelligence to detect and remove terror-related content (Bickert & Fishman, 2017). However, completely blocking ISIS' Internet access is unlikely to succeed in any meaningful way because its members are actively disseminating its promotional propaganda materials on diverse online platforms such as mobile apps and the Dark Web; therefore, defeating the group must begin with aggressively refuting its core extremist philosophy. In this respect, cultural and ideological resistance from the MENA region itself is crucial to counter ISIS' hateful and supremacist ideology. Previous studies have shown that some local and regional initiatives that relied on humor and comedy were effective (Al-Rawi, 2016), including the use of mobile video games (Al- Rawi & Jiwani, 2017). This kind of cultural rejection of extremism includes using the popular term Daesh (داعش) to refer to the terrorist group which is an indirect way to demean and discredit ISIS.

Up until the present day, the centralized media apparatus of ISIS and its propaganda are still active and strong even though the actual Caliphate ended up mostly as a virtual one (Clarke & Winter, 2017). This is another reason why studying different online platforms is important because researchers can understand the new ways by which jihadist propaganda is being disseminated and shared.

As other researchers have similarly concluded, terrorists and their sympathizers always find alternative methods and even platforms to post propaganda on social media and elsewhere. For example, justpasteit.com (Milton, 2016) and Archive.org are among the most popular alternative websites that are still routinely used by ISIS to upload their jihadist videos, pamphlets, books, and images. More recently, encrypted mobile apps, such as Telegram, offer the terrorist group the ideal personalized means to stay connected with its followers and sympathizers, share updated news, and collect cryptocurrency funding. As ISIS has lost its control over land in the Middle East (Warrick, 2017), the actual and most fierce war is happening now more virtually and much less on the front line.

Future research needs to take into account the above-changing media landscape with a clearer focus on the multilayered use of mobile apps, the Dark Web, and cryptocurrencies. This needs to include using more advanced digital forensic methods to trace cryptocurrency funding, especially on Monero, as well as employing better technical means and open-source intelligence tools to understand cross-platform dissemination of jihadist propaganda, especially between the Dark Web and Telegram, on the one hand, and the surface web such as Archive.org and traditional social media sites such as YouTube, on the other hand. So far, the most stable and secure online space for ISIS remains the Dark Web due to the difficulty of identifying jihadist content and websites as well as the anonymity that the Tor browser affords. Ironically, the ongoing presence of these Dark Web sites, their daily updates, and dissemination of multilingual propaganda can be used as a branding and recruitment strategy to suggest that ISIS remains (باقية) a virtual active 'state', at least in the minds of its followers. In other words, there needs to be a more holistic and effective strategy to limit and counter the dissemination of propaganda by ISIS and its sympathizers, which can be attained if joint government, tech companies, researchers, journalists, and public efforts are merged.

References

Al-Rawi, A. (2016). Anti-ISIS humor: Cultural resistance of radical ideology. *Politics, Religion & Ideology*, *17*(1), 52–68. https://doi.org/10.1080/21567689.2016.1157076

Al-Rawi, A., & Jiwani, Y. (2017). Mediated conflict: Shiite heroes combating ISIS in Iraq and Syria. *Communication, Culture & Critique*, *10*(4), 675–95. http://dx.doi.org/10.1111/cccr.12177

Bickert, M., & Fishman, B. (2017, November 28). Hard questions: Are we winning the war on terrorism online? Facebook Newsroom. https://newsroom.fb.com/news/2017/06/how-we-counter-terrorism/

Calamur, K. (2016, February 5). Twitter's new ISIS policy. *The Atlantic*. www.theatlantic.com/international/archive/2016/02/twitter-isis/460269/

Clarke, C., & Winter, C. (2017, August 17). The Islamic State may be failing, but its strategic communications legacy is here to stay. War on the Rocks. https://warontherocks.com/2017/08/the-islamic-state-may-be-failing-but-its-strategic- communications-legacy-is-here-to-stay/

Greenberg, J. (2015, November 21). Why Facebook and Twitter can't just wipe out ISIS online. Wired. www.wired.com/2015/11/facebook-and-twitter-face-tough-choices-as-isis-exploits-social-media/

Milton, Daniel. (2016, October 10). *Communication breakdown: Unraveling the Islamic State's media efforts.* Combating Terrorism Center at West Point. /www.ctc.usma.edu/v2/wp-content/uploads/2016/10/ISMedia_Online.pdf

Warrick, J. (2017, August 18). ISIS's propaganda machine is thriving as the physical caliphate fades. *The Washington Post.* www.washingtonpost.com/world/national-security/isiss-propaganda-machine-is-thriving-as-the-physical-caliphate-fades/2017/08/18/4808a9f6-8451-11e7-ab27-1a21a8e006ab_story.html?utm_term=.39156f2d9196

Index

Note: Endnotes are indicated by the page number followed by "n" and the note number e.g., 36n4 refers to note 4 on page 36. Page locators in **bold** and *italics* represents tables and figures, respectively.

For Product Safety Concerns and Information please contact our EU
representative GPSR@taylorandfrancis.com
Taylor & Francis Verlag GmbH, Kaufingerstraße 24, 80331 München, Germany

www.ingramcontent.com/pod-product-compliance
Lightning Source LLC
Chambersburg PA
CBHW050534270326
41926CB00015B/3222

* 9 7 8 1 0 3 2 6 1 5 8 7 5 *